Illegal Immigration

Look for these and other books in the Lucent Overview series:

Abortion	Homeless Children
Acid Rain	Illegal Immigration
Alcoholism	Illiteracy
Animal Rights	Immigration
Artificial Organs	Mental Illness
The Beginning of Writing	Money
The Brain	Ocean Pollution
Cancer	Oil Spills
Censorship	The Olympic Games
Child Abuse	Organ Transplants
Cities	Ozone
The Collapse of the Soviet Union	Pesticides
Dealing with Death	Police Brutality
Death Penalty	Population
Democracy	Prisons
Drug Abuse	Rainforests
Drugs and Sports	Recycling
Drug Trafficking	The Reunification of Germany
Eating Disorders	Schools
Endangered Species	Smoking
The End of Apartheid in South Africa	Space Exploration
Energy Alternatives	Special Effects in the Movies
Espionage	Teen Alcoholism
Euthanasia	Teen Pregnancy
Extraterrestrial Life	Teen Suicide
Family Violence	The UFO Challenge
Gangs	The United Nations
Garbage	The U.S. Congress
Gay Rights	The U.S. Presidency
The Greenhouse Effect	Vanishing Wetlands
Gun Control	Vietnam
Hate Groups	World Hunger
Hazardous Waste	Zoos
The Holocaust	

Illegal Immigration

by Kathleen Lee

LUCENT
BOOKS

323.631
LEE

Library of Congress Cataloging-in-Publication Data

Lee, Kathleen.
    Illegal immigration / by Kathleen Lee.
       p.   cm. — (Lucent overview series)
    Includes bibliographical references and index.
    Summary: Discusses the debate about illegal immigration into
the United States, its economic and cultural effects, and efforts to
deal with the situation
    ISBN 1-56006-171-5 (alk. paper)
    1. United States—Emigration and immigration—Government
policy—Juvenile literature.   2. Aliens, Illegal—Government policy—
United States—Juvenile literature.   3. Aliens, Illegal—United
States—Juvenile literature.   [1. United States—Emigration and
immigration.   2. Aliens, Illegal.]   I. Title   II. Series
    JV6483.L44   1996
    325'.21'0973—dc20
                                  95-24158
                                     CIP
                                     AC

Contents

Introduction

THE BORDER BETWEEN San Diego, California, and Tijuana, Mexico, is the busiest crossing in the world. At the official checkpoint in the San Diego community of San Ysidro, trucks and cars line up to enter the United States. A few border patrol agents keep watch over the people standing on the other side of a ten-foot, solid steel fence. The people on the Mexican side of the border stand, sit, or pace along a levee, awaiting a break in the agents' attention. To get to this point, within spitting distance of the United States, they have crossed a twelve-foot fence, a ditch, a sixteen-foot fence, and the toxic waters of the Tijuana River. Some shake out plastic bags they used to wrap their feet when crossing the river. The two groups of people eye each other suspiciously. Even in the middle of the day, the people waiting to cross the border illegally outnumber the border patrol agents. By the middle of the night the crowd of men, women, and children will grow even larger. Every day of the week the same scene takes place: People wait their turn to join the ranks of illegal immigrants living and working in America.

Meanwhile, some of the foreign travelers who arrive at international airports across America intend to stay in America illegally. Illegal immigrants arriving at JFK International Airport in

(Opposite page) For most illegal immigrants, the journey to the United States is a difficult one. These illegal immigrants descend a homemade ladder to gain entry into the United States.

New York City might use one of several methods to enter the United States illegally. An unknown number of people simply remain in America after their legal tourist visas expire. They find work and a place to live, but their lives are rarely free from worry about being caught and sent home, or deported. Others carry false documents that go undetected by airport customs officials. Still others tear up their tourist visas on their flights to America so that they can claim that political persecution awaits them if they are forced to return to their home countries.

A strong attraction

All of these people—whether they cross at the United States–Mexico border on foot, arrive by boat along America's shoreline, or step off an airplane—are illegal immigrants. Illegal immigrants are people who enter or remain in a country in violation of that country's laws. In America illegal immigrants are also called undocumented workers, illegal aliens, or illegals. Illegal immigrants come to America from many countries, including China, El Salvador, Ireland, Mali, Mexico, Nigeria, Peru, Romania, and Thailand.

Immigrants are pushed from their own countries by economic difficulties and political upheavals and pulled toward America by the possibility of economic opportunities and political and religious freedom. People from all over the world want to immigrate to America. Increased population, poverty, and lack of jobs in the Third World create a growing stream of migrants to the industrialized nations of Western Europe and North America. Conflict and economic disruption in Eastern Europe, Ireland, and the republics of the former Soviet Union also add to the flow of migrants. New communication technology has alerted people even in remote countries to the advantages of life in America. The expansion of transportation options makes it possible for almost anyone to travel long distances.

Most people who want to live in America immigrate legally. America accepts approximately 700,000 legal immigrants per year—more than all other industrialized nations combined. Nevertheless, there are limits to legal immigration, and many who cannot immigrate legally disregard laws and risks and come anyway. It is estimated that between 200,000 and 300,000 illegal immigrants settle in the United States each year. The large number of immigrants, both legal and illegal, coming to the United States causes concern

A proud new citizen waves the American flag during a swearing-in ceremony. Although approximately 700,000 legal immigrants are accepted annually by the United States, it is believed that another 200,000 to 300,000 immigrate illegally each year.

En route to America, Cuban refugees overflow from the decks of the ship Lady Mary. *Many Americans fear that illegal immigrants will cause overcrowding, a lower standard of living, and strain the U.S. economy.*

about the country's capacity to absorb so many people.

Some Americans fear that the influx of immigrants will result in overcrowded cities, towns, roads, and facilities and a decreased standard of living for themselves and for their children. They worry that hospitals, schools, and social service agencies cannot handle the number of people using them, thereby reducing the quality of care, education, and services. They question whether the economy can withstand the arrival of tens of thousands of job seekers when there does not seem to be enough work for the people already in America. Americans concerned about the country's natural resources argue that unchecked population growth from immigration will eventually reduce air quality and compromise the supply of clean water and arable land.

The continued presence of illegal immigrants gives Americans the impression that there is no control along the nation's borders. Their presence also prompts some Americans to feel that their nation's generosity is being abused. President Bill Clinton addressed American concerns about illegal immigration in a 1993 speech when he said, "We will not surrender our borders to those who wish to exploit our history of compassion and justice."

Today, in the mid-1990s, more people want to immigrate to America than America has agreed to accept legally. As Americans struggle to reconcile the benefits and difficulties of hosting a substantial population of illegal immigrants, the challenge of resolving the problems resides with the American people and their politicians.

1

The Legal and Illegal

WHENEVER GOOD JOBS are hard to find, pay is low, and the economy is strained, Americans want to restrict immigration. They worry that newcomers will take scarce jobs, drive wages down, and make life more difficult. This was true even in the first century of America's nationhood.

For example, the nation severely restricted the immigration of Chinese citizens in the late 1800s. Chinese immigrants made up 90 percent of the workforce that built the western section of the transcontinental railroad in the 1860s. Many landowners and employers sought their labor because the Chinese had a reputation for being responsible, hardworking, and willing to accept lower wages. But most Americans in the 1800s were opposed to Chinese immigration. American workers feared that the steady influx of Chinese laborers would take jobs from other Americans and lower everyone's wages. Many believed that the Chinese were too different in appearance and culture to become true Americans. Consequently, in 1882 the United States passed its first law excluding a specific group of immigrants. However, many Chinese citizens found ways around the law, entered the country, and stayed illegally.

(Opposite page) From Ellis Island a young boy points out the Statue of Liberty to his parents. Upon arrival in America, many legal immigrants are inspired by dreams of liberty, yet face resentment from citizens who fear they will take jobs.

By the end of the nineteenth century, the government created the Office of Immigration, later to become the Immigration and Naturalization Service (INS). The federal government began to develop consistent national controls on immigration, and the task of regulating immigration shifted from the individual states to the federal government. The duties of the Office of Immigration included regulating contract labor, monitoring ships that carried immigrants, and deporting those who entered unlawfully. America had established a means to direct and control immigration to its shores.

The Quota Act

The next significant law to restrict immigration was the Quota Act of 1921. After World War I the volume of immigrants increased from the record low numbers of immigrants during the war years. For example, in 1918 only 100,000 immigrants came to the United States, the fewest immigrants in more than fifty years. But 1920 saw the number of immigrants increase by more than 300 percent. The years after World War I also saw an increase in unemployment and housing shortages across America. Many citizens resented having to compete with immigrants for jobs and housing. The Quota Act of 1921 was intended to be a temporary measure to control postwar immigration.

The Quota Act limited the number of immigrants on the basis of national origin. This law gave preference to European groups that had been in America for a long time, such as the English, French, and Scandinavians, and limited the immigration of nonwhites. The quota system, sometimes called the national origins system, had two goals: to reduce the number of immigrants from Eastern Hemisphere countries and to select the nationality of immigrants. Fixed quotas were es-

tablished for each country and allowed more immigrants from nations deemed desirable. The Immigration Act of 1924 made the Quota Act of 1921 permanent.

One unforeseen result of the quota system was an increase in illegal immigration. After implementation of the quota system, immigrants from the Eastern Hemisphere began entering the United States illegally through Canada or Mexico, countries not subject to quotas. After 1917 an increase in the entry tax and a requirement that immigrants be able to read and write encouraged some immigrants to avoid the legal channels and enter illegally. The 1924 act also provided funds to create the border patrol within the Office of Immigration to enforce immigration laws and to

The Immigration Act of 1924 allowed the United States to limit immigration on the basis of national origin. Preference was given to French, English, Scandinavian, and other European immigrants, but greatly limited the immigration of nonwhites.

Mexican laborers participate in the Bracero *guest-worker program in Salinas, California. Established during World War II to overcome labor shortages, the* Bracero *program allowed Mexican citizens to work in the United States for short periods of time.*

cope with the growing problem of illegal immigration. Border patrol agents patrolled the Canadian and Mexican borders and sent illegal entrants back across the border.

When the nation's economy improved and there were more jobs than people, American policies and attitudes softened towards newcomers. For example, to overcome labor shortages during World War II, the government instituted the *Bracero* guest-worker program in 1942. Under this program the government invited people to work in the United States for short periods of time. The *Bracero* program established a pattern of people coming north from Mexico for work. In fact, most of the *Bracero* participants came from Mexico; they took jobs working in the fields of California and Texas. In 1959, the peak year of the program, 500,000 workers were admitted.

In 1952 more than 500,000 immigrants were caught trying to enter the United States illegally. The 1950s brought a variety of legislation aimed at controlling illegal entries. For instance, law enforcement officers were empowered to search vehicles suspected of carrying illegal aliens. In 1954 the border patrol ran "Operation Wetback," rounding up and deporting more than one million undocumented Mexican migrant workers, as well as some U.S. citizens who were mistaken for illegal aliens. Illegal immigration increased sharply when the *Bracero* program was canceled in 1965.

The Immigration and Nationality Act

The Immigration and Nationality Act of 1965 replaced the quota system with numerical limits. It gave preference to family members of citizens or permanent residents, rather than determining an applicant's status on the basis of national origin. In 1968 the first numerical limits were established for Western Hemisphere countries. Although Americans have been willing to accept a wider variety of immigrants with fewer and less racist restrictions, there has been no significant decrease in the number of illegal entries since the mid-1960s. The U.S. government has struggled to prevent undocumented workers from coming into America, but immigrants determined to work and improve their lives come, despite their lack of proper papers.

The U.S. government has increased legal immigration with the hopes of reducing the numbers of people immigrating illegally. The Immigration Act of 1990 allowed 700,000 legal immigrants to enter the United States annually until 1994 and 675,000 to enter each year thereafter. The figure excludes refugees, who number another 125,000 per year. The 675,000 level consists of 480,000 family-sponsored immigrants, 140,000 employment-based immigrants, and 55,000 "diversity immigrants" from countries that were excluded under previous immigration laws such as the Quota Act. Refugees are allowed into the United States without going through the regular immigrant visa process.

To become an American citizen a legal immigrant, or permanent resident alien, must go through a process called naturalization. Naturalized citizens may vote, hold government jobs, and travel freely with a U.S. passport. Only 37 percent of legal immigrants apply for citizenship, partly because it is a complex process. All resident aliens who work must pay taxes, whether they are citizens or not.

How illegal immigrants come to the United States

It is difficult to count the population of undocumented workers in the United States accurately because most of these workers avoid contact with official agencies for fear of deportation. The

Of the thousands of immigrants who enter the United States legally each year, only an estimated 37 percent apply for citizenship. Once immigrants complete the citizenship process they are sworn in as U.S. citizens.

current best estimates are that between 2.5 and 4 million illegal immigrants live and work in the United States with about 200,000 to 300,000 additional illegal immigrants settling here each year.

Forty percent of the illegal immigrant population probably enters through airports. People with tourist visas initially enter as legal tourists. However, if they stay on after their visas have expired and find work and a place to live, they become undocumented workers. They were authorized to visit the United States, not live and work here. In recent years the number of visa overstays from Ireland and Eastern Europe has tripled. Because they are harder to track and because they are primarily Caucasian, they garner less attention. "Who's the illegal alien? He's the guy with the briefcase sitting next to you on the plane, or the cute blond au pair girl who runs off to California two weeks after she arrives here," says a U.S. Customs official.

Others arrive at airports with false visas that go undetected. Illegal immigrants who enter on forged documents or overstay their visas are often well educated or have specific job skills. These are the illegal immigrants who can create competition for jobs with Americans. They are looking for a better life here, and they "are more sophisticated and more likely to take those good jobs that US citizens would want because they have skills," explains Mike Flynn, INS chief of enforcement for the western region. Those undocumented workers who come through airports are harder to apprehend because they do not cluster in border areas where there are large numbers of border patrol agents. "Once you're here, you're here, basically for as long as you feel like it. And all the Border Patrol agents in the world can't stop it," said one U.S. Customs official.

Still other arrivals claim political persecution in their home countries and ask for political asylum once in America. Under current U.S. law these claims are subject to review, but the backlog is such that the review process can take ten years or more. Meanwhile, claimants are released onto the streets of America and may never appear for their hearings. When they fail to appear, but remain in the country, they become illegal immigrants.

Risky land crossings

The majority of illegal immigrants cross into America by land, either walking or driving across the six thousand miles of border shared with Canada and Mexico. Some make the journey alone; many enter with the aid of a smuggler or group of smugglers. In Spanish these smugglers

Signs along freeways in San Diego County alert drivers to the possibility of people crossing busy thoroughfares. During a two-year period, nearly 250 illegal immigrants were struck by cars on San Diego's Interstate 5.

are called *coyotes* and their human cargo of illegal immigrants is called *pollos*, chickens, or sometimes *mojado*, wet, because the journey from Mexico frequently entails crossing a river. Chinese smugglers are known as snakeheads. The smugglers charge large amounts of money for their services, and there is no guarantee that the journey will be a success. An illegal immigrant from mainland China might pay anywhere from $15,000 to $35,000 for the journey to America. An illegal immigrant from Mexico will pay between $300 and $500 for a basic journey over the border. The deluxe border crossing from Mexico can cost as much as $5,000 and includes travel by air, temporary residence in a safehouse, English lessons, and assistance finding jobs. As many as 45 percent of the illegal immigrants who arrive by land cross the border at or near San Diego. On any given day Armenians, Chinese, Irish, Sudanese, Poles, and many other people are apprehended on the United States–Mexico border.

Smugglers and groups of immigrants risk bandits, capture and detention by the border patrol, and vehicular accidents. In July 1987 eighteen Mexican men suffocated inside a sealed boxcar in the desert of West Texas because they were too frightened of being deported to call for help. Interstate 5 in California is called *El Calle Muerte*, the highway of death, by Mexicans and "slaughter alley" by Americans. Nearly 250 men, women, and children were struck by cars on Interstate 5 in San Diego County in a two-year period. There are many other dangers as well. By the time illegal immigrants arrive in the United States, 65 percent have been robbed, extorted, beaten, or raped by bandits or the Mexican police. Some immigrants choose to cross sections of remote desert rather than take the risks of entering densely populated areas immediately. This type of journey carries the dangers of water deprivation and getting lost or spotted by border patrol planes. "Yes, it's dangerous, but Mexico offers us nothing but misery," says Luis Lopez, a migrant agricultural worker.

A harsh journey

Large expanses of coastline surround the United States. In recent years increasing numbers of illegal immigrants have tried to enter the United States by ship. Between 1991 and mid-1993, U.S. authorities observed more than forty vessels carrying illegal immigrants toward North America. About half of those were intercepted. Still, the ships continue to come. "We can't send our people, like Barbary pirates, out to interdict vessels on the high seas. Meanwhile, they're coming from every direction, every ocean—the

Pacific, the Atlantic, the Caribbean. There are too many oceans, too many ships," said Jack Shaw, head of investigations for the INS. Most of these ships are commissioned by Chinese smugglers. However, the INS knows of smugglers from Pakistan and India as well.

In June of 1993, Americans suddenly learned how harsh and dangerous these journeys often are. The *Golden Venture,* an old ship never meant for open ocean travel, was filled with Chinese citizens hoping to immigrate to America. It had traveled a circuitous seventeen-thousand-mile route from Hong Kong through Thailand, Singapore, Kenya, and finally to New York. The conditions aboard the ship were appalling; there was little freshwater, little room for the nearly three hundred passengers, and not enough food. The ventilation was poor and the journey took many

The freighter Golden Venture *ran aground off Rockaway Beach in Queens, New York, in June of 1993. Its Chinese passengers endured terrible conditions in hopes of gaining entry to the United States.*

days longer than expected. "We brushed our teeth with saltwater. Twenty days, that's how long they said the voyage would take. But it was long, so bitter, so hard," said one passenger. Finally, due to a failed rendezvous with fishing boats that were to carry the passengers to American shores, the ship ran aground off Rockaway Beach in Queens, New York. In a mad scramble passengers jumped ship and began swimming ashore in the icy water. Six people died and the rest huddled on-shore, shocked and saddened by this strange ending to a terrible journey.

Like most immigrants to America, even illegal immigrants expect life to be wonderful once they arrive; they expect to find work easily, earn a lot of money, and grow rich and comfortable. "In Mexico, everyone talks about America. You can get work easily, there's lots of money, they say. It's all lies," said Ricardo Valle from Mexico who has learned that the myth of riches in America is not always true.

Ricardo Valle came to America from Mexico illegally when he was sixteen years old.

An emergency medical worker examines illegal Chinese immigrants who reached the American shore after a harrowing seventeen-thousand-mile journey.

> I traveled to the (border) in Tijuana, where I met a group of 12 and a *coyote*. We paid the *coyote* $300. It took us about an hour to cross Diablo Canyon. In the middle, we were robbed by bandits. After the border we came to a very busy road, which all of the immigrants had to cross, where a lot of people get hit by cars. We got caught by the INS. They took us back to Tijuana. The next day the *coyote* met us again and we crossed again. I almost got caught again, but I managed to somersault through a hole in the fence. The patrolman was too busy catching the other six people to go after me. The *coyote* took two of us to a house near the border where we hid. Early the next morning a car came and took us to LA. Then I got on a bus to San Francisco, where I had a friend.

Illegal immigrants from Mexico are believed to account for 30 percent of the illegal immigrant population. Thirty-seven percent come from Central and South America and the Caribbean. At least one-third of illegal immigrants are not from Mexico or Latin America. Authorities estimate that the current population of illegal immigrants residing in the United States includes one million Mexicans; 300,000 El Salvadorans; 120,000 Guatemalans; 100,000 Canadians; 100,000 Poles; and 100,000 Filipinos.

A willingness to risk everything

Each illegal immigrant has his or her own story of success and failure, of hardship, danger, and fear. There are as many ways to cross the border as there are people who do it. The immigrants share a determination to come to America and a willingness to risk everything to achieve that goal. "It doesn't matter how many people, horses, bicycles, helicopters or planes they use. People will go. It doesn't matter if the fence is electric," says Javier Ortega of Guadalajara, Mexico.

Many Americans assume that illegal immigrants are uneducated, unwilling to learn English, and reluctant to assimilate. English language classes, however, have waiting lists. Eighteen of forty finalists in the 1991 Westinghouse high school science competition were foreign-born children of foreign-born parents. In Boston thirteen of seventeen public high school valedictorians in 1989 were foreign-born students. Many of these people are illegal immigrants or the children of illegal immigrants. Susan Lee, a Korean florist in Los Angeles, says, "I would like to ask Americans clamoring about illegal immigrants to be a little more tolerant. We're not all uneducated and undesirable people who are draining American taxpayers."

Since early in its history, America has sought to control the numbers of people who immigrate

to its shores with laws and enforcement agencies. At the same time America has the most generous legal immigration policy of any country in the world. Yet, despite this determined effort, illegal immigration continues. The difficulties of entering the United States illegally do not deter the legions of illegal immigrants.

Despite laws and stepped-up enforcement efforts, immigrants continue to enter the United States illegally.

The Incentives to Illegal Immigration

IN VENTURA COUNTY, California, men begin to gather in an empty parking lot before sunrise. These men are the migrant workers, many of whom are here illegally, who support California's lucrative agriculture industry. The men stand along the road, hoping to catch the eye of one of the employers driving past slowly in pickup trucks.

A similar scene takes place at many street corner lots around Los Angeles where men wait for an employer to pick them up for a day's work gardening, laying carpet, or painting. This is one part of the informal economy that relies on illegal immigrant workers. The workers are undocumented, and the work they do is undocumented, that is, it occurs outside government regulations. This part of the American economy could be called uncharted; it exists mainly on a cash basis, sidestepping a paper trail of bookkeeping, reports, and forms.

Garment workers in New York City or Los Angeles are often illegal immigrants who work long hours for very low pay in substandard conditions. Employers frequently take advantage of undocumented workers because the workers are too frightened of being caught and deported to speak up about workplace infractions such as no overtime pay, no breaks, and no benefits. Also, many workers do not speak much English and are unaware of workers' rights in America.

In New York City's Chinatown an illegal immigrant may work three different jobs: the breakfast shift at one restaurant, lunch at another, and dinner at a third. Working fourteen-to-sixteen-hour days and living in a small apartment shared with as many as eight others makes for a frugal life. However, the net pay in one month is three times more than one year's net pay in China.

Freedom and opportunity

Illegal immigrants come to America to work. They come because there are more job opportunities here. They work hard and frequently hold as many jobs as they can physically handle. They can change cities or jobs whenever they feel like it. They can think and say what they please; they

Undocumented workers gather on a Los Angeles street corner to solicit employment.

can attend whatever church they like. They can educate themselves. America offers a lifestyle that few countries in the world have: political freedom and economic opportunity.

While economic opportunities in America are often significantly greater than in other countries, many immigrants are unaware of the difficulties they will face in achieving their dreams of success. According to Patricia Fernandez-Kelly, a sociologist at Johns Hopkins University:

> Their perspective is one of, "what do I have to do to survive and support my family? I don't mind selling ice cream in the street or cooking food at home and selling it on the corner if that's what's necessary to pull myself up by the bootstraps." . . . Immigrants all think they're going to be the next Donald Trump, even when there's plenty of evidence that their belief is not warranted.

The possibility that there is the chance to make it big, no matter how remote that chance is, is enough to draw people to America to seek their fortunes.

For illegal immigrants, the chance to work and to live in a democracy is strong incentive to make the journey to America. Says Los Angeles business consultant Jose Legaspi:

> The people on the street come from another country, and they want a job—any job. They may get minimum wage, or even less, but it's a lot more money than they've ever had before. In other countries, a lot of times, they would work for worse wages all their lives, and that's it. There's nothing to learn and no way to learn it.

Economic disparity

There is very little economic opportunity in the countries that give birth to many of America's illegal immigrants. Farmers in China earn $173 a year while city dwellers earn about $367 yearly. Although expenses are lower, most people agree that these earnings leave very little room for growth or improvement. "It was impossible to get ahead," explained Wang Huoshui, an illegal immigrant. Liu Sui, another Chinese immigrant, said, "It's hard to work here. But it's even harder to live in China." The difficulty of life in their home countries prepares many illegal immigrants for the difficulties they will face as undocumented workers in America. Working fourteen-to-sixteen-hour days at several jobs, Chinese immigrants can make nearly $1,000 a week in America. By sharing close living quarters to keep their expenses low, many Chinese illegal immigrants are able to save 80 percent of their incomes.

The average wage in Mexico is about 60 percent lower than in the United States. The per capita income in Mexico is $2,165 yearly, com-

The difficulty of life in their home countries often prepares illegal immigrants for the long hours and hard work they will endure as undocumented workers in the United States.

pared to nearly ten times that level in the United States. A day's wages repairing tires, Luis Lopez's profession in his hometown in Mexico, cannot buy one pound of meat. In 1992 forty-four million Mexicans were considered impoverished; 40 percent of the population was underemployed. Wages had not increased since 1980. More than a million Mexicans enter the workforce each year in an economy that generates enough new jobs for less than a quarter of a million workers. Compare this to the availability of low-paying (by American standards) jobs in agricultural and service industries just over the northern border. Although a typical wage for illegal immigrants in America might be less than $3 per hour, this is still far better pay than what they can earn at home, especially when there is the opportunity to work several jobs and long hours. Other countries are even less prosperous than Mexico, and many economies are crumbling from recession and instability. The U.S. economy is still one of the strongest in the world. With such dramatic economic differences it is no wonder that people try to come to the United States any way they can. Even the lowest economic rung here is better than life in many other countries.

Chances and choices

Pablo, an undocumented worker from Mexico, comes from a town that has fifty houses, all without running water or electricity, and no local high school. The only jobs available are farmwork or raising livestock, both of which pay poorly. There was no reason for him to stay. Pablo dreamed of coming to America, finding a job, having a home, and sending money to his family in Mexico. "I choose to be here. Illegally," he says. In Los Angeles Pablo works ten to eleven hours a day in a laundry without overtime pay, benefits, or sick leave. He studies English when he can and hopes one day to work with computers or in a hotel.

> All we want are opportunities to work . . . and to get to know the United States and its people. Here, a person has chances and choices. You can go to school. You can learn to be a mechanic. You can learn to be a teacher. You can have a business. You can do so much.

Realities of working illegally in America

Not every illegal immigrant has a positive experience in the American job market. Many are surprised by the prejudice and exploitation, the low wages, and the difficulties of finding work. They feel that the least appealing jobs are available to them, but Americans do not appreciate their doing these jobs that Americans will not take. They struggle to live and work in a country whose language they do not speak or understand. They are confused by strange customs and exhausted by long hours of work.

"The pay is incredibly low and the hours are incredibly long," says John Lum, program director for the Chinese Staff and Worker's Association in New York City. One garment worker worked for thirty-six hours straight only to have pay docked for taking a one-hour nap. Nonpayment of wages is common, and a group of thirty-five garment workers accumulated more than $120,000 in unpaid back pay. "They are slaves, pure and simple," says a U.S. immigration official.

Jose Chaveza is returning home after three years in Los Angeles. "The American dream is not true. It didn't happen. I have no more dreams. No way to pay the rent." He, like other illegal immigrants, has found the realities of life as an undocumented worker harsh. "I think I will return to Mexico. Every day it is more difficult," says Chaveza.

Asian garment industry workers, many of whom are in the United States illegally, often work long hours for low pay.

Illegal immigrants have discovered that the recession in California and other popular immigrant destinations affects even jobs on the lowest end of the scale. There are more undocumented workers than there is work available. "Street-corner labor markets have become overpopulated relative to the demand," explains Wayne A. Cornelius, director for the Center for U.S.–Mexican Studies at the University of California at San Diego. For some it is not possible to stay on here without work, and they return home.

Others would like to return home, but cannot. Noemi is an unemployed illegal immigrant from Mexico. She says:

> I don't like it here. I don't want to live here. I want to be with my family. But now, we don't have the financial ability to return. We came here to try our luck and to see if everything we heard is true. It's

not true. Here, a person who does not work does not eat. And it's hard to find work. We didn't come here for welfare. One comes here to work, not to get things for free. You feel badly. You know you can do something, but simply for the reason you are not a legal resident you cannot work.

Those who have work accept the long hours and low pay. Ana Maria, a Salvadoran immigrant who works for piecework rates in the garment industry, averages about $3 an hour. "Who else would hire me? I don't speak English. I'm not educated. All I can do is work hard." But she does not resent her position. Ana Maria and her husband, together, make between $200 and $300 dollars weekly. They share a one-bedroom apartment with two other Salvadoran immigrants. Their only extravagances are regular calls home, and every few months they manage to send $50 to $100 home to their parents. And still, they live better than they did in El Salvador.

The seven members of the Barrera family, also from El Salvador, shared an apartment with seven other relatives for three years in New York City while the father earned $30 a week making furniture and the mother worked as a house cleaner. The mother began making *pupusas* and *tamales* at home and selling them to her Central American neighbors for extra money. As demand increased, the children began working with her as well. After 1986 the family became legal residents when the U.S. government offered an amnesty to all illegal immigrants then residing in the States. The Barrera family rented a small space for their first restaurant, and they were in business. Now there are five Barrera restaurants, one run by each child, providing jobs and good food to many people. The Barrera family, like many illegal immigrants, came to the United States asking only for the chance to work. They turned their chance into a success.

Immigrants, both illegal and legal, come to America to make a better living than they could in their home countries, to improve their lives and provide a better life for their children, to find religious and political freedom, and to escape war. The immigrants who come here illegally are often driven by a natural instinct to improve themselves; they are self-sufficient, hardworking, resourceful, and determined to succeed. "For the rest of the world, the American dream is just to live in America. I live here now. So I know it's real," says Antonia, a Mexican woman who works as a domestic worker in San Diego. "America is a land of opportunity, if you work. But you have to work. I left Mexico because I had no chance to better myself [in Mexico]," says Salvador Espinoza, who owns a vegetable processing plant in Salinas, California, and a ranch and hotel in Jerez, Mexico.

Illegal immigrants are willing to take the risks of coming here illegally in order to improve their lives. "Alone or with a *coyote*, it's a risk you must take to get good work," Pablo says.

Immigrants come to the United States seeking the American dream. Determined to make a better life for themselves and their families, immigrants are often hardworking and self-sufficient.

3

Illegal Immigration's Economic Impact

(Opposite page) Many American businesses and industries, from farming to construction to garment manufacturing, benefit from cheap, undocumented immigrant labor. Low wages allow many American companies to compete with inexpensive imports from countries that also offer low pay to workers.

IN THE SPRING of 1993 President Clinton's first and second choices for attorney general, Zoe Baird and Kimba Wood, stepped down from consideration for the job after disclosing that they had hired undocumented workers to care for their children. During a time of widespread economic hardship, the public was outraged by evidence of well-to-do, upstanding members of the legal profession breaking the law and providing jobs for illegal immigrants. In response to the criticism, Zoe Baird said that she was doing what was best for her children. The assumption was that she could not find a legal resident to do that job as well, for the right pay. The conclusion is that illegal immigrants fill a gap in the American economy. Many citizens and experts disagree strongly with this premise. What is at issue is whether illegal immigration helps or hurts the U.S. economy.

Although economists and other experts disagree on exactly how illegal immigration affects the economy, they do agree on a few facts: Illegal immigrants are a source of cheap labor, they pay some taxes, and they use some social services.

Illegal immigrants provide a pool of cheap labor. For example, Chinese garment workers in New York City work a sixty-hour week for $200 or less, and do not receive health or other benefits. Few legal workers in America would accept such wages and conditions of employment. Because of their illegal status, undocumented workers are generally willing to accept any job they can get at whatever pay is offered. Because they rarely have good English language skills, they more often have difficulty finding well-paying jobs. Undocumented workers accept jobs in garment factories, as domestic helpers, manual laborers, and harvesting crops—work considered undesirable by many legal residents and citizens. For example, a 1993 San Diego County study found that illegals work primarily in private yard landscaping, construction, agriculture, factories, shops, automotive services, and restaurants. All

With only minimal English language skills, undocumented workers often have difficulty finding well-paying jobs. They tend to work in areas that depend upon manual labor, such as yard work.

of these jobs require little English, few skills, and hard work. Illegal workers provide a flexible, low-cost labor pool for U.S. companies, thus allowing local companies to compete with inexpensive imports from cheap-labor countries.

Taxes, social services, and the illegal immigrant population

All illegal immigrants pay state sales and excise taxes. The range of these taxes varies from state to state, but can be found most often on food, gasoline, and household goods. Like other state residents, illegal immigrants pay taxes on their purchases. Some illegal immigrants also pay state income and payroll taxes. The 1993 San Diego County study estimated that 54 percent of employed, undocumented workers had taxes withheld from their pay. The county also estimated that illegal immigrants generated $59,722,384 in annual state and local tax revenues.

Some illegal immigrants work with false social security numbers and pay federal taxes associated with possessing a social security number. The San Diego County study estimated that "Approximately one-third (33.3%) of undocumented immigrants utilize false documentation for employment or other purposes, with up to a 50.0% false documentation factor being a distinct possibility." The study stated that undocumented workers in San Diego County paid $162,632,543 in federal taxes annually.

Illegal immigrants generate costs in the areas of public education, health services, and criminal justice. Illegal immigrants of school age have the right to attend public school. All illegal immigrants have the right to receive emergency medical treatment, whether or not they have the money to pay for it. Additionally, illegal immigrants arrested on criminal charges move through the criminal justice system with attendant court, attorney, and incarceration costs, like any legal resident.

Education, health, and crime

Education costs represent the highest outlay for illegal immigrants. This expense is picked up by states. School districts in communities with large illegal immigrant populations say the presence of so many children who do not speak English as their first language is a burden because these students often need extra help and attention and many state educational systems are already underfunded and overpopulated. In San Diego County, for example, 13,310 undocumented students attend public school, accounting for 3.3 percent of the total enrollment.

Health care is another area where illegal immigrants receive benefits. Federal and state laws require hospitals to treat anyone who is seriously ill, meaning that poor, uninsured illegal immigrants can receive free care. Although illegal immigrants are generally reluctant to seek medical care because they fear deportation, they do go to clinics or public hospitals for severe illness. Delayed care often leads to more serious illness, which then requires more expensive treatment. "Only the most desperate will resort to seeking health care from the county hospitals . . . usually under conditions where they are so ill they have no choice," says Linda Wong, a former attorney with the Mexican Legal Defense and Education Fund. As the cost of health care rises and the funds available for public assistance shrink, local officials are reluctant to pay for medical care for illegal immigrants. A 1992 Los Angeles County study estimated that a quarter of all patients in the public hospital and clinic system are illegal immigrants, and that two out of three births are to illegal immigrants. The births alone are estimated to cost California taxpayers $60 million a year. Illinois officials estimate their state spends $54 million annually on health care for undocumented workers.

Illegal immigrants charged with crimes have the right to legal representation at public expense. They have a right to trial by jury and can pursue

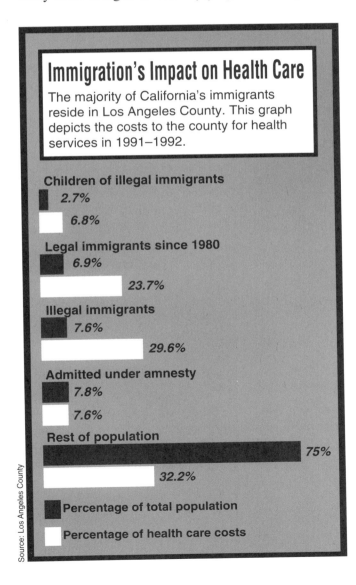

Immigration's Impact on Health Care

The majority of California's immigrants reside in Los Angeles County. This graph depicts the costs to the county for health services in 1991–1992.

Children of illegal immigrants
2.7%
6.8%

Legal immigrants since 1980
6.9%
23.7%

Illegal immigrants
7.6%
29.6%

Admitted under amnesty
7.8%
7.6%

Rest of population
75%
32.2%

Percentage of total population

Percentage of health care costs

Source: Los Angeles County

all judicial appeals. If convicted, they serve their sentences in state or federal prison. The U.S. Bureau of Prisons estimates that more than 25 percent of inmates in federal prisons are illegal immigrants; 15 percent of the California state prison population are illegal immigrants. The state of California is believed to spend at least $500 million a year to house, feed, and care for illegal immigrant inmates. Illinois officials estimate their expenditures on illegal immigrant criminals at $44 million annually.

Illegal immigrants are not eligible for unemployment compensation, social security, or most other social service benefits. However, the American-born children of illegal immigrants are, by law, American citizens, and they are eligible for Aid to Families with Dependent Children, public housing, and Medicaid. Laws regulating use of social services by illegal immigrants vary from state to state and are inconsistent and full of exceptions. Some illegal immigrants use loopholes in the laws or inaccurate assessment of legal status to receive welfare, food stamps, unemployment benefits, or disability insurance.

A question of costs and benefits

Because the debate over illegal immigrants and their economic impact lacks precise statistics and facts, many conclusions are more theory than fact. The debate generally centers around two issues: whether or not illegal immigrants take jobs from Americans or contribute to the economy by creating jobs and businesses and whether or not their financial and tax contributions match their social service costs.

The question of costs and benefits of illegal immigrants involves complex financial analysis. Few organizations or individuals are free from bias. One organization might think that illegal immigrants help the economy and that is what its study will conclude, while another organization might believe that illegal immigrants hurt the economy and its findings will most likely confirm this view. "As with all accounting exercises, one's assumptions effectively determine the answer," writes George Borjas, an economics professor at the University of California at San Diego.

Experts disagree on whether illegal immigrants take jobs from legal residents and American citizens, although most agree that undocumented immigrants work at jobs that Americans do not want. "Even if consumers and the economy in general benefit from lower product costs and

While experts argue about the economic impact of illegal immigration, most agree that undocumented workers obtain jobs that Americans do not want. These undocumented workers have found work picking grapefruit in Phoenix, Arizona.

lower fuel prices. . . in certain parts of the country . . . people may be pushed out of jobs," says Charles Keely, a migration expert at Georgetown University.

U.S. businesses that employ low-paid, unskilled, undocumented workers undermine the benefits won by American workers, such as the minimum wage, eight-hour workday, and pensions. In addition, a large, unskilled, undocumented population of workers encourages businesses to remain labor intensive and to postpone mechanization in favor of cheap labor. The short-term benefits of cheap labor may prevent the United States from competing successfully in the global economy in the long run.

More than their fair share?

States with the largest populations of illegal immigrants claim they carry a disproportionately heavy financial burden. California is the destination of nearly 50 percent of all illegal immigrants. Five other states absorb most other illegal immigrants: Florida, Texas, New York, New Jersey, and Illinois. These are the states where the effects of illegal immigration on the economy are most apparent. Taxpayers and politicians in these states pay more than their share of the bill for illegal immigrant expenses and have begun to demand economic relief from the federal government.

In fact, 4 percent of the states' residents are illegal immigrants. Officials in these states say that illegal immigrants cost their states millions of dollars, and in the case of California billions of dollars, that should go toward improving the lives of legal residents and citizens. State officials argue that the federal government should pay for services to illegal immigrants because the federal government is responsible for immigration policies and enforcement.

In 1994 California, Florida, New York, Texas, Arizona, and New Jersey all sued the federal government for reimbursement for services provided to illegal immigrants. California demanded more than $3 billion. Florida sought $750 million. New York estimated it spent $800 million a year on illegal immigrants. The states argue that immigration laws and enforcement of those laws all turn on decisions and policies of the president, Congress, and various federal agencies. The states feel that the federal government should bear the burden of borders that remain porous, especially because the federal government benefits from taxes paid by undocumented workers. The intention of these lawsuits, even if they don't produce financial reimbursement, is to highlight the issue of illegal immigration and to illuminate the financial concerns of the states most strongly affected.

Florida's lawsuit was dismissed in December 1994; California's suit was dismissed in February 1995. In dismissing the California lawsuit, U.S. district judge Judith Keep stated that there is no legal precedent for a state suing the federal government for failing to enforce immigration laws. California governor Pete Wilson vowed to take the case to the U.S. Supreme Court and also to use political power to "ensure that California taxpayers are no longer burdened with picking up the cost of the federal government's failure to secure the border."

A strain on the economy

Some studies support the states' claims that illegal immigration hurts their economies. In a 1993 study commissioned by the Carrying Capacity Network (CCN), an organization supporting population stabilization and resource conservation, Donald L. Huddle, a professor of economics at Rice University, concluded that

California sued the federal government in 1994 for reimbursement for services provided to illegal immigrants. Governor Pete Wilson stated that California taxpayers should not be burdened by "the cost of the federal government's failure to secure the border."

illegal immigrants who had settled in California since 1970 cost $18.2 billion more than the $8.9 billion they paid in taxes.

In another 1993 study California state senator William Craven of San Diego and the California Special Committee on Border Issues detailed the fiscal impact of illegal immigration on San Diego County. "Our primary aim is to gather data which can be used to petition the federal government for reimbursement of services to the undocumented which have been unfairly borne by state and local taxpayers," said Senator Craven in his introduction of the study. The study concluded that the net annual cost of illegal immigrants in San Diego County was $244,287,699.

Undocumented workers help the U.S. economy

Some economists and experts suggest that far from hurting the U.S. economy, illegal immigrants make vital contributions to it. They argue that illegal immigrants increase job opportunities for all Americans by spending their earnings on the output of other workers. Although their earnings might be low, they buy food, clothing, household products, appliances, and other consumer products. They earn and spend money like everyone else in America. Additionally, illegal immigrants' acceptance of low-paying jobs keeps goods priced at competitive levels. American consumers enjoy lower prices on everything from clothing to restaurant meals because of the lower wages paid to illegal immigrants.

For example, the California agriculture business is one-tenth of the state's economy. In 1993 statistics indicated that at least half of the one million agricultural workers were illegal. As the percentage of illegal agricultural workers increased, hourly wages fell from $5 or $6 to $4.25 or less, without benefits. With the fall in wages, growers changed to more labor-intensive crops like strawberries, which are too soft for machinery and require two thousand person-hours an acre to harvest. Strawberries are now a significant crop in central California. Growers argue that U.S. consumers are accustomed to cheap produce, and one way to keep costs low is to employ undocumented workers.

In the manufacturing sector, the differences in wages are evident from a 1994 study conducted by the International Textile, Garment and Leatherworks Federation, the International Labor

Organization, and the U.S. Bureau of Labor Statistics. The study compared wages in athletic footwear factories. Legal workers in America earn between $7.38 and $7.95 hourly. Wages in Thailand for the same work range from 65 cents to 74 cents hourly, and in China the wages range from 10 cents to 14 cents hourly. The higher wages paid to legal American workers means that American companies are less competitive on the world market. An hourly wage for illegal garment workers in sweatshops in New York City or Los Angeles might be as low as 65 cents or as high as $3. "Without illegal immigrants, many US factories would go offshore. The garment industry in East Los Angeles . . . would be in Taiwan or Mexico," said Douglas Massey, a sociologist at the University of Chicago.

Strawberries are now a major crop in central California. Growers contend that they can keep costs low for this labor-intensive crop only by hiring undocumented workers.

The problem, some experts claim, is not that illegal immigrants hurt the economy by their presence, but that their costs, in social services for example, are not evenly balanced by their benefits. Most of the taxes paid by illegal immigrants go to the federal government while most of their expenses are paid at the state and local levels. This uneven distribution makes it appear that they are actually a strain on the economy. "In a macro sense, any economist will say, immigration—even illegal immigration—is always a gain to society. The problem is a distributional one. Taxes flow to the federal government, but services used are at the state and local levels," says Charles Keely of Georgetown University.

Not much of an effort

San Diego economics professor George Borjas calculates that the amount of money on both the cost and benefit sides is insignificant. He concludes that illegal immigration has no serious financial impact on the American economy, either positive or negative. "At the national level, therefore, it would not be farfetched to conclude that immigration is a near wash-out," says Borjas.

Many experts argue that immigration, legal or illegal, brings economic growth, more wealth, and progress for all Americans and is, therefore, of general benefit to society. The increased demand for housing, groceries, and other necessities helps the economy, and employers invest their expanded profits in new machinery and more jobs. "It's called competitive capitalism, and it works. It's how America got rich," says Tony Carnavale of the American Society for Training and Development.

In growing economies immigration increases the demand for housing, food, and services, and generally improves job opportunities for low-skilled native-born workers. Lawrence Fuchs, a

Brandeis University professor and former executive director of the U.S. Select Committee on Immigration and Refugee Policy, says his research convinced him that illegal immigrants "probably create more jobs than they take away." In 1994 the Urban Institute published the results of a study concluding that immigration, both legal and illegal, has little overall effect on jobs for native-born Americans. "Overall the job displacement effects are trivial," says Michael Fix, one author of the Urban Institute's report.

The difficulty of weighing costs and benefits

Illegal immigrants often begin new businesses, contribute to the overall vitality of the economy, and create jobs. Many illegal immigrants are highly motivated workers; they often invest their savings in projects calculated to improve their lives and the lives of their children. They buy and renovate undesirable land or buildings, thus creating jobs as well as improvements. Immigrant-owned-and-supported businesses create jobs and pay taxes. For example, Susan Lee came from Korea and now owns a florist shop.

> I brought my life savings to Los Angeles and I've been living off it mostly. I contribute to the economy of Los Angeles and California by spending money here. . . . Most undocumented Koreans are like me—they have their own businesses. They do not use government services. Not a thing.

Although the debate over the effects of illegal immigration on the U.S. economy is likely to continue with opposing sides compiling statistics to support their views, several facts are clear. Illegal immigrants provide American businesses with cheap labor. Illegal immigrants pay taxes in varying amounts. Illegal immigrants receive benefits in the forms of public education, emergency health care, and their use of the criminal justice system. Some illegal workers manage to obtain social service benefits for which they are not technically eligible, such as welfare and unemployment insurance. States with significant populations of undocumented workers pay more of the costs of illegal immigration than does the federal government. Despite numerous studies and reports, there is still no clear answer to the question of whether or not the benefits of illegal immigration outweigh the costs.

4

Backlash

WORDS ENGRAVED ON the pedestal of the Statue of Liberty proclaim, "Give me your tired, your poor, your huddled masses yearning to breathe free. . . ." Despite these words, Americans have alternated between recruiting and resenting immigrants. In the nineteenth century when America received hundreds of thousands of immigrants, those who had already settled here often treated the newcomers with resentment, suspicion, and disdain. New immigrants were typically blamed for economic hardship, scarce jobs and housing, and low wages. They were accused of not assimilating into American life. Americans believed the newcomers did not learn English well enough or fast enough and retained the habits of their former countries long after they should have become "American." Americans used and abused the immigrants. For example, Chinese laborers were needed to work on the railroads, and later excluded from immigrating. Immigrants from Ireland, Italy, and southern and eastern Europe were all viewed as suspicious and unappealing. An editorial in the May 15, 1880, edition of the *New York Times* claimed, "There is a limit to our powers of assimilation, and when it is exceeded the country suffers from something very like indigestion." Issues of race and difference combined with economic

(Opposite page) The Statue of Liberty welcomes immigrants to the United States, offering freedom and opportunity to those who wish to stay. American citizens, however, often shun newly arrived immigrants—legal and illegal.

53

troubles to create a sometimes powerful backlash against newcomers.

Another backlash against illegal immigrants has been building in the 1990s. The American economy has not been strong, and some Americans respond to illegal immigrants in their midst with the same resentment, suspicion, and dislike that previous generations felt toward legal immigrants in the nineteenth century.

Californians approve Proposition 187

The state of California has made one of the strongest public statements on the topic of illegal immigration. In November 1994 voters approved an initiative that denies access to public education, nonemergency health care, and other social services to the state's approximately 1.3 million illegal immigrants. The initiative, called Proposi-

tion 187, was approved by 58.8 percent of California voters. Californians who voted for Proposition 187 were convinced that the cost of illegal immigration was sending their state into financial ruin. "We are a generous people. But there is a limit to what we can absorb and illegal immigration is now taxing us past that limit," said California governor Pete Wilson. Wilson is one of the proposition's strongest backers.

Proposition 187 requires health and education officials—nurses, doctors, teachers, and social workers—to verify immigration status before providing any but emergency health care or before allowing a child into a classroom. They must report to federal immigration authorities anyone they reasonably suspect of being an illegal immigrant. Many nurses, doctors, and teachers are unwilling to perform this law-enforcement role. They do not believe that public schools, hospitals, and clinics are appropriate places to enforce federal immigration laws, nor do they believe that they are the appropriate people to act as immigration agents.

Proposition 187 makes the possession or sale of false social security cards or false resident-permit cards a felony punishable by up to five years in jail. "If they are in possession of a fraudulent green card, they've committed a felony in the state of California, and we expect the law will be enforced," says Ron Prince, one of the authors of Proposition 187.

Legal challenges filed

Despite the nearly three-to-two victory margin at the polls, the initiative has been held up in court. All of Proposition 187's provisions but one—the ban on the sale and use of fraudulent immigration documents—have been blocked indefinitely in state and federal courts. The Los

Hundreds of students protest California's Proposition 187. The proposition would deny illegal immigrants access to public education, nonemergency health care, and other social services.

Angeles, San Francisco, and Sacramento school districts, along with some individuals, filed suit to halt implementation of the measure. They contend that each of their districts could lose up to $650 million in federal funds if they are compelled to verify the immigration status of students and their parents because such actions violate federal policies. This claim has been supported by Richard Riley, U.S. secretary of education. He has warned California that its school districts could lose more than $2.3 billion in federal assistance if Proposition 187 goes into effect because schools are barred, under the Family Education Rights and Privacy Act, from disclosing information about their students for law-enforcement purposes.

Individuals and elected officials in both San Francisco and Los Angeles are challenging the constitutionality of the measures in the initiative in both state and federal courts. Challengers assert that the initiative violates individual rights to privacy, as well as rights to education and health care.

Objections to restricting access to public education have an especially strong possibility for success. The courts have already spoken on granting all children the right to public education. A 1975 Texas law to withhold educational funds for children not "legally admitted" into the country was challenged in the courts. It was invalidated by the 1982 Supreme Court decision in *Doe v. Plyler* that all children, regardless of immigration status, have the right to public education. The opinion written by Justice William J. Brennan Jr. noted that public education was not a constitutional right. However, "neither is it merely some governmental 'benefit' indistinguishable from other forms of social welfare legislation." Brennan wrote that education has "a fundamental role in maintaining the fabric of our society." Denying children access to education runs the risk of adding to unemployment, welfare, and crime. The costs of public education, including school meal programs and bilingual and special education programs, are considerable. Nevertheless, under the 1982 decision, every child in the United States, whether here legally or not, has a right to attend public school.

Other restrictions sought

Although the future of Proposition 187 is uncertain, citizens of other states with large illegal immigrant populations are watching the events in California closely. Groups of citizens in New York, Florida, and Arizona are planning their own versions of Proposition 187.

California governor Pete Wilson has also urged passage of a constitutional amendment that would

Carrying the Mexican flag and signs that read "No human is illegal," high school students in Berkeley, California, protest Proposition 187. Many opponents contend that the proposition is based on racism rather than on economic factors.

deny citizenship to U.S.-born children of illegal immigrants. Section one of the Fourteenth Amendment to the U.S. Constitution states, "All persons born or naturalized in the United States, and subject to the jurisdiction thereof, are citizens of the United States and of the State wherein they reside." If U.S.-born children of illegal immigrants are denied citizenship, they cannot legally receive social service benefits including Aid to Families with Dependent Children, Medicaid, and low-income housing. Wilson wants to limit state expenditures on illegal immigrant families by prohibiting their U.S.-born children from becoming citizens and receiving the benefits that accompany citizenship.

Some people claim racism is the driving force behind Wilson's proposed constitutional amendment and measures such as Proposition 187. Racism can be found at the heart of some of the backlash against illegal immigrants. Some citizens object to nonwhite, non-European, non-Christian immigrants, legal or illegal, coming to the United States in economically good or bad times. Some experts believe that racism is the most significant factor in an anti-immigrant backlash. "Some people genuinely worry about the problem of too many immigrants in a stagnant economy. But for most, economics is a diversion. Underneath it is race," says Bill O. Hing, an immigration expert at Stanford Law School. Many immigrants experience racism. And many white Europeans who are undocumented workers in the United States go unnoticed because to many Americans an illegal immigrant is someone from Mexico, Central America, or Asia.

What about those who wait their turn?

Illegal immigration is indeed a complex issue. Racism may be a factor in how some citizens feel about illegal immigration, but it is not entirely responsible for the current backlash. For example, some Americans strongly object to people benefiting from life in America by breaking the laws. Illegal immigration does not seem fair to Americans who point out that there is a way to come here legally. Why should illegal immigrants be allowed privileges that are denied to those immigrants who wait patiently, sometimes for years, for the legal right to come to America? Tens of thousands of petitioners await entry visas. To allow those who come illegally to stay is to send the message that anyone who waits his or her turn is a fool. Americans feel immigrants should respect U.S. laws and procedures in coming to America. "To ignore this crisis of illegal immigration . . . is not only irresponsible, but makes a mockery of our laws. It is a slap in the face to the tens of thousands who play by the rules and endure the arduous process of legally immigrating to our country," California governor Pete Wilson said in an April 1994 address.

Health and safety worries

Changes experienced in communities with large populations of illegal immigrants have also contributed to the backlash. For example, 45 to 50 percent of all illegal entries into the United States occur in San Diego, California, a city on the United States–Mexico border. It hosts a significant population of illegal immigrants, both temporary and permanent. The city and county feel the strain of a population of illegal immigrants estimated at 220,000. Illegal immigrants make up 7.9 percent of the total population of San Diego County.

San Diego County residents resent changes in their community as a result of illegal immigration. Makeshift communities have sprung up in empty lots and canyons, and become home to several hundred people. Many local residents express concern about health and public safety. Citizens worry that a significant population living in substandard housing, with inadequate sanitation, nutrition, and health care, could result in the rapid spread of communicable diseases. Joyce Stiffler of Carlsbad had more than a dozen Latino men camped within ten yards of her back fence. "What bothers me is the health problem. I feel like we're fighting a losing battle. The Board of Health came in here last year and cleaned one bunch out, and now they're back again. . . . Do we feel threatened? You bet we do."

Citizens' concerns about the potential spread of diseases is well founded. Infectious disease ex-

Border patrol agents lead a group of illegal immigrants to a processing area after their capture and arrest in San Diego, California. Approximately 45 to 50 percent of all illegal entries into the United States occur in San Diego County.

perts say that communicable diseases are on the rise in communities with high populations of illegal immigrants due in part to inadequate preventive care for illegal immigrants. Children are not vaccinated against deadly and contagious childhood diseases. Adults do not seek treatment until they are seriously ill. Health providers argue that ignoring illegal immigrants or prohibiting them from receiving health care is not the solution. Dr. Juan C. Ruiz works at a public health clinic in Los Angeles. He says:

> For us to think we can ignore the health care needs of undocumented immigrants, it's a farce. Illnesses don't recognize borders or barriers and if we deny health care to undocumented immigrants we will create a public health hazard because by denying health care to them we're denying illnesses can be contagious.

Makeshift migrant camps

With so many undocumented immigrants in their midst, communities cannot cope with the increased burden on public schools and local health clinics. Communities also face an increase in crimes such as auto theft and burglary, resulting from a large population of underpaid or underemployed illegal workers. A citizens committee in Poway, a city in San Diego County, reported on the illegal immigrants in its community, "We are in a refugee (like) situation, but without normal assistance given to refugees, such as temporary housing, medical relief, legal aid and relocation assistance."

The largest migrant camp in San Diego County is called Rancho de los Diablos. The existence of the camp has brought many angry San Diegans to city hall to demand that the knot of shacks be torn down. Other residents have called for public funds to improve living conditions in the camp. The camp is home to nearly five hundred people, many of whom are illegal. Portable toilets provided by the Catholic Church are heavily overused and neglected. Garbage is strewn everywhere, there is no safe source of water, and shacks are made from every conceivable scrounged material. The buildings are fire hazards; the sanitation is far below standard; and officials, for the most part, stay away from the camp and its problems.

Kevin McNamara, a commercial real estate broker, thinks that there is no hope of improving life in the camp and that it should be razed. He is concerned for the safety of people who live in such unsanitary, unsafe conditions, as well as the safety of legal county residents. As he sees it, to allow residents of the camp to live in such conditions is worse than to raze the camp. "It's almost racism to let this happen. We're allowing a group

Members of the San Diego Urban Corps help clean up refuse at Rancho de los Diablos, the largest migrant camp in San Diego County. The makeshift community houses nearly five hundred migrants, many of whom are illegal.

San Diegans participate in a "Light Up the Border" rally to help curb illegal immigration. Participants hoped to impede border crossings while also publicizing the problem of illegal immigration.

of people to live outside the rules that govern everybody else," said McNamara.

One group of angry San Diego County residents, some of whom live in houses directly on illegal immigration routes into the United States, decided to hold a public protest against illegal crossings. About once a month in 1989 and 1990 hundreds of San Diegans drove to the United States–Mexico border to shine their headlights into Tijuana in a series of "Light Up the Border" rallies. Their goal was to impede the crossing of illegal immigrants, publicize the increasing problem of illegal immigration, and show that it was possible to make it harder for immigrants to cross the border illegally. Muriel Watson, founder of a group called Light Up the Border, which has since disbanded, and organizer of the rallies, said,

"I call it the silent invasion. The hemorrhage of Mexico into the United States."

Results of backlash

America's history of reacting strongly against newcomers during times of economic hardship continues, and Americans are especially unwelcoming toward those who come illegally. Some Americans believe the only way to stop illegal immigration is to prevent illegal workers from creating a life in America. If illegal immigrants cannot send their children to school or receive treatment when they are ill, perhaps they will not enter the country. Communities with large illegal immigrant populations object to the changes brought about by their presence. Californians expressed their reaction to illegal immigrants in their state by voting to restrict illegal immigrants' access to public services. Americans often fail to consider whether a backlash against illegal immigrants might affect their lives as well. The hidden costs of not providing adequate health care or education to illegal immigrants may be considerable. Some experts point out that measures like Proposition 187 will only create a greatly impoverished, unhealthy, outlaw underclass. According to Emily Goldfarb, director of the Coalition for Immigrant and Refugee Rights and Services in San Francisco:

> People need to understand the phenomenon of global migration. Immigrants come here because of conditions in their home countries, for reasons having to do with politics, economics and war. . . . No one really believes that, if we take away all their rights and services, that will change immigration.

5

The Border Patrol

THE IMMIGRATION AND Naturalization Service (INS), as part of the Department of Justice, is the branch of the federal government responsible for overseeing and enforcing immigration laws. The INS has four main areas of responsibility: facilitating entry of people legally admissible as immigrants or visitors to the United States; granting benefits under the Immigration and Nationality Act, which includes providing assistance to those applying for political asylum, temporary or permanent resident status, or naturalization; preventing illegal entry, employment, or receipt of benefits; and apprehension and removal of illegal immigrants.

The border patrol is an enforcement division of the INS. The border patrol's main responsibility is to keep the international boundaries secure and to detect and prevent smuggling and unlawful entry of illegal aliens. Additionally, the border patrol has acquired responsibility for pursuing criminal aliens and interdicting drugs and other contraband crossing the border.

The border patrol is responsible for managing about 19,500 miles of land border and coastline. To successfully manage these areas, the border patrol is divided into four regions: northern, eastern, western, and southern. Each region is divided

(Opposite page) A border patrol agent in Nogales, Arizona, arrests three undocumented migrants. Under the authority of the Immigration and Naturalization Service, border patrol agents are authorized to apprehend and deport illegal immigrants.

into three to seven sectors, based on topography, routes of travel, and the potential for illegal immigration traffic. Border patrol strategies consider terrain features, transportation facilities available to incoming illegal immigrants, and nearby employment opportunities. Through the early 1990s, the border patrol's principal enforcement techniques have included line and river watch, sign cutting, city patrol, farm and ranch check, traffic check, boat patrol, air operation, and crewman control.

Enforcement techniques

Line and river watch is the most prevalent border patrol technique. Border patrol agents literally patrol, on foot or in vehicles, the land or river border, especially crossing areas most popular with illegal immigrants. The goal is immediate apprehension and prompt removal. Agents often work from hidden positions, follow up leads, and respond to information delivered by electronic sensors; aircraft and observation tower sightings; or tracks, marks, and other physical evidence. Deterrence, or preventing illegal immigrants from attempting to cross the border, has been of secondary concern; apprehension and removal after unlawful entry is the primary concern.

Sign cutting refers to tracks, marks, and physical evidence. When on sign-cutting duty, border patrol agents track signs left on the ground by people passing through. This technique is used in areas not controlled by line-watch assignments. "Drag trails" keep the ground smooth so agents can detect prints. Generally this technique is used in conjunction with air support. A ground crew tracks border crossers while an air crew spots them and directs the ground crew to their location.

Agents conduct traffic checks along the highways and side roads frequented by illegal immi-

grants; the agents stop vehicles and check the immigration status of the passengers. City patrol involves checking businesses that employ unskilled or semiskilled workers, as well as checking public transportation hubs to detect illegal immigrants traveling from place to place within the United States by bus, train, and airplane. Boat patrol covers the rivers that run along the international border, large lakes, and coastal areas. The goal and procedure is similar to line watching. Farm and ranch checks apprehend illegal immigrants who evade the first line of defense along the border and manage to get jobs inland. Aircraft patrol the international borders, looking for people walking over and away from the border, and report any sightings of illegal immigrants to ground crews. Crewman control seeks to apprehend foreign-ship crew members who desert at U.S. ports. The border patrol utilizes airplanes,

By patrolling highways and side roads frequented by migrants, border patrol agents have been successful at apprehending illegal immigrants.

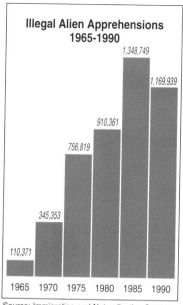

Illegal Alien Apprehensions 1965-1990

Year	Apprehensions
1965	110,371
1970	345,353
1975	756,819
1980	910,361
1985	1,348,749
1990	1,169,939

Source: Immigration and Naturalization Service.

helicopters, motor vehicles, sophisticated surveillance equipment, fences, and high-tech lighting in its fight against illegal immigration.

Despite border patrol efforts to stop illegal immigration, illegal crossings continued at a high rate in the mid-1980s. In 1986 the border patrol apprehended 1,767,400 people illegally trying to enter the United States. While this number sounds impressive, immigration experts estimate that many more people escape notice and successfully cross the border. "The general rule of thumb is that for every one caught, three or four get across," says Ernesto Rodriguez, an immigration expert at the University of Houston.

Congress tries legal reform

In response to the steady rise in illegal immigration, Congress passed the Immigration Reform and Control Act (IRCA) in May 1986. The IRCA was the most comprehensive immigration reform attempt in two decades. It was the first law that addressed illegal immigration as an issue separate from general immigration policy. The IRCA allowed longtime illegal residents in the United States to obtain legal status. It was also designed to punish employers for hiring undocumented workers.

The IRCA prohibits the employment or recruitment of workers who are in the United States illegally. It requires that employers verify the legal status of all workers when they are hired. Employers caught hiring undocumented workers are subject to employer sanctions, that is, a series of fines.

Border patrol agents help in the enforcement of the IRCA; they review hiring practices and detect violators of the IRCA.

In the first couple of years following passage of the IRCA, the number of illegal immigrants apprehended at the border fell, reaching a low of 954,243 in 1989. Since 1989, however, apprehensions of illegal immigrants have risen. The border patrol apprehended 1,258,482 illegal immigrants in 1992, for example. Generally, lower numbers indicate fewer people crossing and higher numbers indicate more people crossing. The illegal immigration situation "has returned to business as usual. Those who delayed migration in the past are now coming, having observed that work is still available even for new arrivals lacking papers," says Jorge Bustamante, president of the College of the Northern Border in Tijuana, a center for immigration research.

Operation Hold the Line

The increase in apprehensions has prompted the border patrol to reassess its techniques and change its methods. The border patrol changed its focus from apprehension and removal to deterrence in two sectors, El Paso and San Diego. In these sectors the border patrol's goal is to deter illegal immigrants from crossing the border, rather than trying to catch them after they cross. The first experiment began in September 1993 when Operation Hold the Line, as it was named, was launched in El Paso. "We're not playing the numbers game anymore, of seeing how many people we can catch. We're concentrating on keeping people out," said Doug Mosier, spokesman for the border patrol in El Paso.

Of the twenty-two border sectors nationwide, the El Paso sector is the largest geographically and the second busiest. A three-mile section of the El Paso border is the most active spot for border crossings. The El Paso sector employs 665 agents who patrol 125,500 square miles, 121,000 in New Mexico and 4,500 in Texas. Nearly 1.3 million illegal immigrants were apprehended in the El Paso sector from 1989 to 1993. About 40 percent of those apprehended had made the long journey from the interior of Mexico or from Central America. About 60 percent came from the border city of Juarez. Fifty percent of the El Paso sector apprehensions occur during daylight hours, and El Paso is the destination for 70 percent of those apprehended.

Under Operation Hold the Line, El Paso's 240 agents were divided into groups of about 50 agents, each working ten-hour work shifts. The agents are dispersed along a twenty-mile border area. Each agent is responsible for patrolling an area of approximately one-half mile. The stand-out feature along this part of the United States–Mexico border is the broad Rio Grande, which provides a natural barrier between the two countries. Flat desert, irrigation ditches, and sparse brush characterize the rest of the area. This

After illegally crossing into El Paso, Texas, from Juarez, Mexico, a family waits for the opportunity to cross an area that is carefully watched by border patrol agents.

type of terrain permits a single border patrol agent to effectively control a relatively large section of the border. The agent can easily spot people trying to cross illegally and move to intercept them. At the same time, people trying to cross can clearly see the agents waiting for them on the other side. This visible deterrent has discouraged many would-be illegal crossers.

Operation Hold the Line has resulted in a 70 to 75 percent decrease in apprehensions and a marked decrease in congestion, loitering, and crime in the El Paso area. From approximately 1,000 apprehensions a day, agents now make about 200 to 250 apprehensions daily. The decrease in apprehensions generally means that fewer people are attempting to cross the border.

Immigration and border patrol officials consider Operation Hold the Line an example of how illegal immigration can be stopped, or at least dramatically slowed. The key is having sufficient personnel and technical resources. "With a sufficient show of force you can stop it. With enough manpower and technology, you can do it humanely and adequately," says Mike Hance, an agent who has worked for fourteen years along the Tijuana–San Diego section of the border.

Operation Gatekeeper

The success of Operation Hold the Line in El Paso encouraged officials to try a similar change in focus, from apprehension and removal to deterrence, in the San Diego sector. Differences in terrain and types of illegal entries between the San Diego and El Paso sectors have resulted in the development of a different style of prevention strategy for the San Diego sector.

San Diego is the largest sector in terms of personnel, where approximately twelve hundred agents are employed, and it is the busiest. In San

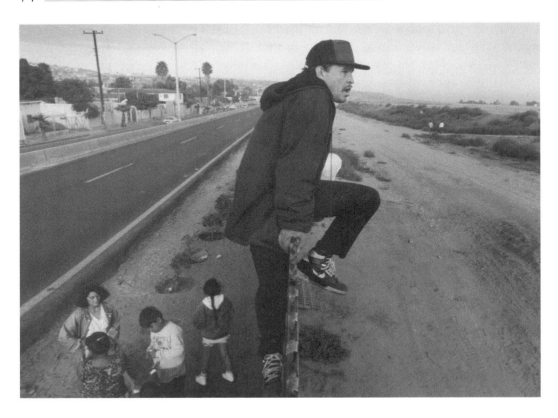

The border along San Diego and Tijuana lacks natural barriers, thus allowing easy access into the United States. In many locations, immigrants can gain illegal entry by simply hopping a fence.

Diego the border lacks natural barriers; an immigrant has only to hop a fence to enter the United States. Once past the border, however, the terrain is mountainous with river valleys, deep ravines, canyons, and heavy brush. This type of terrain provides good cover for illegal crossers and complicates the job of the border patrol. Illegal immigrants make heavy use of a fourteen-mile section. The San Diego sector sees 50 percent more illegal entries than El Paso on a daily basis: Since 1989 three million illegal immigrants have been apprehended in the San Diego sector. Ninety-nine percent of illegal immigrants apprehended in the San Diego sector have traveled long distances from the interior of Mexico or from Central America. Only 1 percent live in the border cities of Tijuana, Tecate, or Mexicali. In the San Diego sector, 85 percent of apprehensions occur at night and 95 percent of the crossers are bound for cities beyond San Diego.

Operation Gatekeeper began in the San Diego sector in the fall of 1994. It makes use of physical barriers, lighting, and large numbers of agents. Fences ranging from ten to sixteen feet in height are set two and three deep in places with a twelve-foot metal sheet underground to prevent tunneling. High-intensity lights reduce entries and make arrests easier. There are plans to install more lights to channel illegal entrants to areas with more open terrain or where the border patrol agents can occupy high ground. Prevention tactics in the San Diego sector include various technologies: Infrared scopes detect illegal border crossers, advanced sensors alert agents to movements and the size of groups of people, and video systems monitor borders from remote sites. Additionally, the staff has been expanded to thirteen hundred agents. In the fourteen-mile section that receives the most illegal entries, two hundred agents patrol constantly during the hours of darkness, when the vast majority of crossings occur. The agents form three tiers of patrol between the border and San Diego. If the illegal crosser isn't apprehended by the first tier, the second or the third tier will probably stop him or her.

Border patrol statistics showed a 3 percent decrease in apprehensions by early 1995. Apprehensions numbered 212,836 between January and April 1994 before the start of Operation Gatekeeper and 205,829 during the same months of 1995 after the program's beginning.

Unintended side effects?

In the San Diego sector, one goal is to redirect the flow of immigrants to less populated areas that are easier to patrol. For example, the area along Imperial Beach is very popular with illegal immigrants because it is close to Tijuana and downtown San Diego where it is easy for illegal immigrants to disappear into crowds and hard for agents to pursue them. On the other hand, a person could walk for eight hours before reaching a populated area in the isolated mountains to the east. This terrain gives agents more time to pick up the illegal immigrants. Some experts question the benefits of this strategy. "You are rechanneling the flows. What difference does it make if you push it to Texas and Arizona? It's sort of like putting a boulder in a stream," says Wayne Cornelius, director of the Center for U.S.–Mexican Studies at the University of California at San Diego.

Experts also point out that increased obstacles such as fences, lights, sensors, and more agents on duty may have unforeseen side effects. Some experts express concern about increased power and business for smugglers and a greater risk of violence between smugglers, illegal immigrants, and border patrol agents. As crossing becomes increasingly difficult, people who previously crossed on their own may seek the services of smugglers, and smugglers will raise their prices as demand and difficulty increases. "The more we fortify, the more we increase their business. It would be enriching a binational mafia of people smugglers that has been roundly condemned by both governments," says Wayne Cornelius.

Smugglers could use the mountains east of San Diego, which are currently favored by drug runners because of the difficult terrain. Border patrol agents would not be able to distinguish between smugglers of drugs and smugglers of people, which could lead to an increase in violence. Illegal immigrants who try desperate new methods or even violence in their attempts to cross the border might expose themselves to new dangers. "In the desperation to cross, if the traditional routes are blocked, perhaps some would commit violence against agents of the border patrol," says Victor Clark Alfaro, head of the Bi-National Center for Human Rights in Tijuana.

The advantages of prevention

Congress established the U.S. Commission on Immigration Reform in 1990 to examine immigration laws and policies and recommend more effective implementation of them. In its 1994 interim report, the commission supported the new

To prevent illegal immigration in the San Diego sector, border patrol agents use infrared scopes (pictured) to detect illegal border crossers.

strategies of Operation Hold the Line and Operation Gatekeeper.

> Prevention holds many advantages: it is more cost-effective than apprehension and removal; it eliminates the cycle of voluntary return and reentry that has characterized unlawful border crossings; and it reduces potentially violent confrontations on the border.

The commission recommended increased government resources—new technology, more fences, and additional staff—to prevent illegal border crossings. It also recommended formation of mobile rapid response teams to improve border patrol response to new crossing and smuggling sites.

The border patrol and violence

Some border patrol activities have created controversy. Complaints of unnecessary violence on the part of border patrol agents have come to public attention. Border patrol agents have been accused of brutalizing people they encounter in their work. In 1993 the human rights group Americas Watch accused the Justice Department of failing to sufficiently investigate hundreds of brutality complaints lodged against border patrol agents since 1989. The organization's report included interviews in which people recounted incidents of beatings, racially motivated verbal assaults, rough physical treatment, unjustified shootings, and sexual abuse and torture committed by border patrol agents.

For example, on January 7, 1992, four border patrol agents caught Roberto Dueñas Guerrero crossing the border. According to a witness, one of the agents kicked the immigrant and broke one of his ribs. The agent pushed Dueñas's head into dirty water, forced him to drink it, and called him "Mexican dog" and "pig." On June 30, 1992, a

Human rights organizations have accused the border patrol of unnecessary violence. This man displays bruises he says he received after his arrest by the border patrol.

border patrol agent in El Paso beat three women, one of whom had papers authorizing her to be in the United States. In June 1993 an agent in a canyon near Nogales, Arizona, shot an illegal immigrant in the back. The agent, Michael Elmer, hid the wounded man, Dario Miranda Valenzuela, rather than calling an ambulance. The victim might have lived had he received proper medical attention. The Immigration Law Enforcement Monitoring Project of the American Friends Service Committee documented 1,274 abuses by the border patrol from May 1989 to May 1991.

Some illegal immigrants claim they have been charged with crimes they never committed. Americas Watch suspects the border patrol of trying to cover up brutality by charging illegals with crimes. The report stated:

> INS agents are aware that most abused migrants, because of their unprotected status, unfamiliarity with English, US law and culture, and fear of deportation will not defend themselves against trumped-up charges and will, instead, accept deportation or other offered plea bargains rather than pursue complaints against abusive agents.

Border patrol agents are the only law enforcement agency along the border. On any given shift, agents may encounter people trying to cross illegally, smugglers leading people across, drug traffickers, and other individuals whose intent is to steal from and attack those who are waiting to cross the border. Some of these people are not

A border patrol agent confronts a group of young people who rob migrants crossing into the United States at Nogales, Arizona.

armed, but some may be armed and desperation may make them dangerous. In the El Paso sector in 1993 agents encountered seventy-two armed individuals; thirty-seven encounters involved narcotics. "I'm down here talking to the people all the time. There is a high number of criminals coming across too. . . . If you try to apprehend a guy and he tries to knock your teeth out, he's probably a criminal," says Alan Summers, a border patrol agent.

"Mainly a peaceful relationship"

Border patrol policies clearly state that agents may use physical force or violence only in self-defense, in defense of another person, or when force is absolutely necessary to make an arrest or prevent an escape. Border patrol officials contend that agents follow agency policies and treat people they encounter with fairness. Alan Summers reports:

> I don't know how many times I've given away my lunch to (illegal immigrants). There's not a border patrol agent out there who doesn't feel sympathy for these people. We know they are just doing what they got to do to better their lives. But we can't just tear the fence down and say come on over. Some people may not like it, but somebody's got to try to maintain control (at the border). It's mainly a peaceful relationship.

Chris Sale, acting commissioner of the INS in 1993, responded to the problems detailed by the Americas Watch report. He emphasized that agents of the INS and border patrol are committed to protecting human rights and to enforcing immigration laws in a humane and fair manner. He found that most of the recommendations made by the Americas Watch report referred to regulations and policies already in place. "However, we acknowledge that room for improvement exists in certain areas and agreed with some of the recommendations found in the report," Sale said. These areas included the procedures for filing complaints against the INS and border patrol for physical or civil rights abuses, the clear identification of agents and agents' vehicles for the purposes of filing complaints, and the policy regarding strip searching people arrested by agents. Sale pointed out that all border patrol agents receive thorough training in agency policies and procedures. Sale pledged to take action against employees who violate human rights and fail to enforce immigration laws in a fair and humane manner.

Improvements can be made

In its interim report, the U.S. Commission on Immigration Reform also addressed the issue of violence and human rights violations within the border patrol. It made four recommendations: more training to enable border patrol agents to respond appropriately to potentially violent situations; improved procedures for judging complaints of border patrol abuses; a means to provide compensation or relief to those subjected to abuses; more effective protection of border patrol agents from violence. The commission stated that strategies such as Operation Hold the Line resulted in reduced violence along the border, "in terms of both reported human rights violations against suspected illegal aliens and attacks on Border Patrol officers."

Border patrol, INS, and other government officials agree that improvement in border management is possible. However, the border patrol will never stop illegal immigration alone. The border patrol can reduce the numbers of people crossing illegally and become more efficient in border control, but as long as there is the possibility of creating a better life in the United States, illegal

immigration will continue. People will accept the hazards of crossing the border illegally if it means they can improve their lives and the lives of their families. Many officials within the border patrol advocate an approach that involves law enforcement along the border combined with political solutions that address economic imbalances, particularly between the United States and Mexico. The North American Free Trade Agreement (NAFTA) is an international trade agreement between the United States, Canada, and Mexico. It is supposed to increase investment in and trade with Mexico, create job opportunities with higher wages in Mexico, and inspire Mexicans to stay in their own country. Chief Agent De La Vina says, "You need strong enforcement and you need. . . some kind of economic reform in Mexico, be it NAFTA or whatever. One thing alone is not going to work. It's got to be a combination."

As long as the possibility of creating a better life exists in the United States, border patrol officials and other experts agree, enforcement measures alone will not halt illegal immigration.

6

Playing the Political Asylum Game

WHEN THE *GOLDEN VENTURE* ran aground off the coast of Queens, New York, in 1993, Americans were moved by the images of the shivering Chinese on the cold beach. When they heard details of the horrific nine-month journey that ended with the icy swim to the beach, some Americans assumed this was another group of illegal immigrants motivated to endure this disastrous journey by dreams of striking it rich in America. Other Americans felt strongly that arriving illegally did not grant them a place ahead of all the other hopeful immigrants following the rules and that they should be sent home to China immediately. In fact, it is unlikely that they were sent back. Most of them probably claimed to be political refugees, not just immigrants hoping for the good life in America. "We risked our lives to come here. I'd rather die than go back," said Zhang Hairong, one passenger from the *Golden Venture*. A claim of political persecution in their home countries grants immigrants the right to a hearing. The current backlog of claims is so huge, and the lack of detention space to hold claimants

(Opposite page) Chinese citizens who came to the United States aboard the Golden Venture *are apprehended by police officers. Many of these illegal immigrants hope to remain in the country by seeking political asylum.*

until their hearings is so drastic, that claimants are released onto the streets and given plenty of time to blend into life in America. Most likely, these Chinese immigrants will never appear for their hearings. For many illegal immigrants, claiming political asylum is equivalent to getting permission to live illegally in the United States.

What is political asylum?

A person seeking political asylum, an asylee, is essentially the same as a refugee—a person unable or unwilling to return to his or her home country because of persecution or the fear of persecution. Anyone may apply for political asylum upon arrival in the United States. The difference between an asylee and a refugee is one of location. An asylee is in the United States or has arrived at a port of entry while a refugee waits elsewhere. The requirements for obtaining asylum are that an applicant have a well-founded fear of ethnic, religious, or political persecution. The Refugee Act of 1980 established that current immigration status, whether legal or illegal, is irrelevant to a claim for political asylum. The Refugee Act removed refugees and political asylees from the immigrant preference system. It set an admission limit of fifty thousand refugees per year, which may be revised by the president and Congress. It also established a procedure for adjusting a certain number of asylees to permanent resident status annually. Individuals who have been granted political asylum may adjust to permanent resident status after one year of continuous presence in the United States.

U.S. immigration policy has long distinguished two types of individuals seeking to come into the country. One is the political refugee and the other is the economic migrant; one is the victim of persecution, the other is in search of greater eco-

"If, on the other hand, you're coming here for economic reasons, you'll have to go back."

nomic opportunities. U.S. immigration law has always been more open to the political refugee, who in the past was usually someone from a communist country. Officials feared a deluge of economic migrants, but they assumed that there were a limited number of political refugees in the world. Since the 1970s, the distinction between the political refugee and the economic migrant has become increasingly blurred. "It used to be clear. Mexicans were economic, Cubans and Vietnamese were political. That changed when the Haitian boat people started coming in the 1970s. Their reasons for leaving were both political and economic. Are they any less endangered than Cubans? Possibly not," INS commissioner Doris Meissner said in 1991. As the line between the political and the economic migrant grew less distinct, U.S. policy became more inconsistent. Any claim for political asylum made by an individual from a communist country—Cuba, the former Soviet Union, Poland, Vietnam—was almost surely accepted. However, during the 1980s large numbers of Central Americans began to flee war and government repression in countries with governments friendly to the United States and seek political asylum in America. Few were accepted as political refugees. For instance, between 1981 and 1986, 18,000 Salvadorans were deported while only 598 were granted political asylum. "Whereas traditionally Cubans and Poles were accepted without significant questioning, Central Americans were grilled and usually not accepted despite the fact that lives were endangered," says Ernesto Rodriguez, an immigration expert at the University of Houston.

The U.S. Coast Guard intercepts Haitian refugees heading for the United States. Unlike some other illegal immigrants, Haitians are considered to be both political refugees and economic migrants.

The sanctuary movement of the 1980s grew out of the inequities of U.S. political asylum policies. Churches and some communities began to offer help and sanctuary to Central American refugees. By 1985 more than two hundred parishes of all denominations were part of the sanctuary movement. In 1989, in response to a lawsuit filed by religious and refugee organizations, the U.S. government agreed to reconsider the cases of tens of thousands of Central Americans whose applications for political asylum had previously been rejected.

Controversy over who is granted political asylum and whose petition is rejected continues to muddle the political asylum process. Since many Third World dictatorships are also poor, every asylum case requires a judgment call as to whether it is genuinely political or merely economic. It is not clear who is eligible for political asylum and who is not. As a result, thousands of people apply in the hopes that they might qualify. The political asylum system is seriously overloaded with a huge backlog of cases. In the process of applying for asylum, many applicants have discovered that holes in the system permit them to stay in America, whether or not they receive political asylum.

How to play the political asylum game

Political asylum is a complicated legal maze. The object, from the American point of view, is to accept those who are truly oppressed. But the maze has left a door wide open for illegal migrants who lack any true claim of political persecution but manage to work the system to their advantage. By lying about their supposed political persecution, these illegal immigrants benefit from a law meant to help genuine political refugees. These false claimants exploit the system for as long as possible and often gain admission into the United States. The first step is to get to the United States by land, sea, or air. If caught by INS agents, a claim of political asylum prevents the INS from starting deportation proceedings. All persons on U.S. soil, whether here legally or not, have the right to seek a judgment of the courts if they feel their individual rights have been violated. A claim of political asylum means that an immigration judge must examine the case.

Asylum claimants are not detained while the INS reviews their claims and schedules their hearing, which may be more than a year away. Asylum applicants have the same constitutional rights as U.S. citizens, and the government gives them temporary work permits. "They get what they wanted right there," says Jack Shaw, an INS investigator. This gives most claimants the opportunity to begin life in America. Pakistani Mir Aimal Kansi, suspected of killing two CIA employees outside agency headquarters in Langley, Virginia, in January 1993, entered the United States on a business visa in 1990. He applied for political asylum, and as his case crawled slowly through the system, he received a work permit, which enabled him to first obtain a Virginia driver's license and then an AK-47 assault rifle. This is a disturbing example of how the system is misused.

Blending into American life

Two-thirds of applicants for political asylum never appear for their hearings, and the INS lacks the resources to track them down and deport them. "That would cost a fortune, and the taxpayers aren't in the mood to increase our budget," says one INS official. Therefore, even if the INS denies the asylum petition, there is very little risk of actual deportation. Claimants simply blend into American life like many other immigrants. Judges only rarely recommend deportation for illegals who have been in the States for at least seven years, so immigrants who fail to appear for their hearings suffer few consequences. "They can play the legal system for over a decade. And while litigating, they form attachments here, so it becomes a catch-22," says former U.S. attorney general William Barr. Even those who break the laws are difficult to deport. Maureen Farrell was an Irish visitor who was arrested for shoplifting in the early 1980s. She asked for political asylum, claiming that she had been in a house bombed by the Irish Republican Army. Appeals kept her case pending for twelve years, after which she was finally deported.

One of the many problems facing the political asylum system is the lack of sufficient detention space for the numbers of individuals in the system now. This lack of adequate space forces the INS to release claimants onto the streets. Between 1988 and 1990, 489,000 illegal immigrants were scheduled to be deported and should have been held while their cases were processed. The INS only

Cuban refugees wave to a U.S. Coast Guard helicopter while floating in the Florida Straits. Cuban refugees who seek political asylum are able to remain in America pending their asylum hearings.

Illegal Chinese immigrants are detained in the El Centro Federal Detention Center in California while their asylum claims are investigated.

had 6,600 beds available. In 1990 only 9 percent of deportable illegals were actually held until they left the country. It costs about $40 a day to detain one illegal immigrant. "We have 62,000 people under (deportation) proceedings in our district and we deport about 750 a year. At that rate it would take 80 years to clear the system out," says Edward McElroy of the INS's New York district.

The political asylum process was designed to protect the rights of legitimate asylum seekers. The cases of those people suffering from true oppression also plod through the overloaded, inefficient system. Officials had no idea that the system created to accept political asylum claims would result in such a backlog. Following passage of the Refugee Act of 1980, officials expected to receive about 2,000 claims annually. In 1989, 101,000 claims for political asylum were filed. "We didn't (expect) the asylum problem.

We thought of it as the ballerina in the tutu saying, 'I defect, I defect,'" says Lawrence Fuchs of Brandeis University. In only one month of 1991, 1,250 foreigners, mainly from Bangladesh, India, and Pakistan, requested political asylum on arrival at New York airports alone. They had boarded flights with false documents that they destroyed en route. Like every other claimant, they were released onto the streets. "The asylum system is broken and we need to fix it," says INS commissioner Meissner.

Frustration over loopholes

Officials are frustrated by the inefficiencies and loopholes in the system. One complaint is that many supposed political asylees "country shop." If their main objective is to flee persecution in their own country, the quickest escape is to go to the nearest friendly country, whether it's Thailand or Kenya. But many political asylees travel through several countries before arriving in the United States to place a claim of persecution. Recent illegal Chinese immigrants are a case in point. The Bush administration issued an executive order to the INS to give "enhanced consideration" to claims of political asylum made by Chinese based on the one-child-per-family policy enforced by the Chinese government. Since the claim that someone is oppressed by this policy is impossible to prove or disprove, 85 percent of Chinese petitioning for political asylum since 1989 have been approved. The Bush policy implies that the threat of abortion or sterilization is akin to political persecution. This means that "even an unmarried 18-year-old who comes out of the hold of a boat and says 'someday I want to have more than one kid'" is potentially eligible for asylum, says Warren Leiden of the American Immigration Lawyers Association. Illegal Chinese immigrants have arrived on

U.S. shores, like those on the *Golden Venture*, after many months of travel through numerous countries, many of which could serve as safe havens from birth control oppression. The truth is, the immigrants do not just want to leave China; they want to come to America.

Proposed changes

Proposed solutions to the backlog of asylum cases are wide ranging. One solution calls for INS officials to verify U.S. visas at foreign airports that are main transit points for passengers en route to the United States. The intent of this plan would be to stop individuals from tearing up documents en route and claiming, without evidence upon arrival in the United States, that they cannot return to their home countries. This plan is viewed as interfering too much in another country's affairs. "How would we feel if Italians wanted to station their immigration officials in our airports checking our citizens' papers?" asks one State Department official.

Another plan calls for the use of summary or expedited exclusion, a system in which INS officials or judges stationed at American ports of entry could review claims on the spot. If the claim appears to have no basis, the individuals could be returned immediately to their country. "We should introduce summary exclusion, what other countries do, to sort out frivolous claims," says INS spokesman Duke Austin. Arguments against this plan point out that it deprives people of due process. However, the abuse of the system is so acute that many officials are willing to overlook a few potential errors in the interest of catching a greater number of false claims. Officials also are in favor of rescinding the Bush order regarding Chinese claims for asylum based on the one-child policy.

INS commissioner Doris Meissner advocates reforms that will combat political asylum abuses and help speed the hearings of legitimate asylum seekers.

In 1994 the INS predicted it would soon have a backlog of 500,000 asylum cases. Reforms in the review process have been proposed to end the abuse of political asylum. Under the proposed changes work permits would be granted only to those whose claims are approved; furthermore, work permits would not be issued until six months after applying for asylum. This would eliminate the problem of false claimants being released onto the streets with work permits. There are also plans to increase the number of immigration judges from 85 to 135 to speed the processing of claims. INS commissioner Meissner says:

> The reforms we propose will preserve fundamental legal protections for legitimate asylum seekers while addressing the problems of asylum abuse. We do not want to close the door on people who are persecuted, but we cannot allow others to take advantage of a process they don't really need or deserve.

Political asylum, established to aid people in fear for their lives in their home countries, has turned into an easy way for illegal immigrants to enter the United States. The system must be reformed to restore its original intentions and to halt the growth of false claims.

7

What Should the United States Do?

ILLEGAL IMMIGRATION SHOWS no sign of diminishing. The world is producing economic migrants and political refugees at an unrelenting rate. Increasing numbers of people desperately want a better life, and they are unwilling to wait for it to come to them. America remains, in the minds of many, a place of great hope and opportunity. If they know they can come here, illegally if necessary, what will stop them? No one contends that illegal immigration is good, but many argue that illegal immigrants deserve to be treated well. Most people agree, however, that everyone would be better served if all immigration was done legally. "The US has the most generous immigration policy in the world—and we should. But you cannot have an immigration policy without enforcing it. There has to be a limit. We cannot sanction lawlessness," says Lawrence Fuchs of Brandeis University.

The Immigration Reform and Control Act

The Immigration Reform and Control Act, passed in May 1986, was an attempt by Congress to stop or lessen illegal immigration. The law granted temporary resident status to nearly three

(Opposite page) An illegal immigrant eludes border patrol agents by hiding near a drain pipe after successfully crossing the border. Efforts to deter illegal immigration have had mixed success.

Nearly three million immigrants who had lived illegally in the United States since before January 1982 were granted temporary resident status under the federal government's amnesty program.

million immigrants who had lived illegally in the United States since before January 1982. The law provided these immigrants with the opportunity to adjust their status and eventually become legal permanent residents with the chance for citizenship. With the resident illegal immigrant population now legal, the other provisions of the act could have a stronger impact on newcomers.

Congress intended for the IRCA to reduce illegal immigration by punishing employers who hire illegal immigrants, thus eliminating the most compelling reason to come to the United States: employment. Through fines, or employer sanctions as they are called, employers would be punished for hiring illegal workers. In 1985 former INS commissioner Alan Nelson noted, "once word spreads along the border that there are no jobs for illegals in the US, the magnet no longer exists." This idea didn't only apply to border crossings. Mike Flynn, INS chief of enforcement for the western region, said, "The basis of the IRCA was if we could stop employment as the magnet, we could stop them from wanting to overstay (their visas)." The IRCA has not worked as planned, and several factors have been cited as reasons for this failure: the absence of a fraud-proof method for checking documents, weak penalties, and lax enforcement.

Employers are required to verify that the people they hire are either citizens or legal immigrants with authorization to work. Potential employees must show proof of their identity, such as a driver's license, and work authorization, such as a social security card, or a "green card." In fact, any two of seventeen documents will prove identity, and the employer need only make a reasonable inspection. Some documents, like birth certificates, have so many variations that it is difficult for employers to know when they are looking at fraudulent papers. The use of false documents to prove identity has become commonplace.

Legal immigrants are required to show their resident alien identification, or "green cards," to gain employment.

The production and sale of false documents has grown into a profitable business. A full 40 percent of undocumented workers are suspected of carrying false papers. In 1992 the INS seized printing presses and more than 250,000 fake ID cards in Los Angeles. A complete package of driver's license and social security card can be purchased for $500 on the streets of many major cities. Even poor-quality fake documents can pass inspection by employers who have no reason to look at them closely. After all, employers are not required to establish the validity of the documents. "The word is out that you can circumvent the law with fraudulent documents. You can pick up a Social Security card for $20 on just about any street corner in Los Angeles," says Duke Austin, spokesman for the INS in Washington.

Because the proliferation of false documents is one reason for the failure of the IRCA, there has been a call for a national ID card to solve the problem. Without tamper-proof identification and authorization documents, the IRCA cannot fulfill its mission. However, Americans have historically opposed a national ID card because they view such identification as an opening to added government control over their lives. "If America were . . . like some Western European nations, we might save ourselves endless inconvenience by establishing a single official ID. Employers could ask to see it, and counterfeiting it would be a serious crime," says Robert Kuttner, economics correspondent for the *New Republic* magazine.

Employers can afford to take the document checking process lightly because the penalties for hiring undocumented workers are almost insignificant. Since 1986 the INS has fined thousands of employers, but the average fine was only $850 per undocumented worker, a small sum for many employers. No employer has gone to jail for breaking the law. A 1991 study by the Select Commission on Immigration and Refugee Policy concluded that about 50 percent of employers disobey the law.

A good method

The INS has sought to address the problems with the IRCA. In 1991 the INS focused its attention on employer sanctions. District offices were directed to spend 30 percent of their time enforcing employer sanctions and 30 percent of their time investigating fraudulent document operations. Employers are investigated randomly in an effort to ensure compliance.

Despite its problems, most officials and experts believe that the IRCA is a good method of controlling illegal immigration. "The (illegal immigration) situation is better than it would have been in the absence of IRCA," says David Simcox, executive director of the Center for Immigration Studies in Washington, D.C.

Recommendations from the U.S. Commission on Immigration Reform

The U.S. Commission on Immigration Reform will issue its final report on ways to more effectively implement U.S. immigration policy in 1997. In its examination of U.S. immigration policy, the commission conducted public hearings, visited cities affected by immigration, and consulted with experts. The commission found that the "immediate need is more effective prevention and deterrence of unlawful immigration." The 1994 interim report concluded, "that the federal government has a responsibility to mitigate the impacts of unlawful immigration on states and localities, particularly through renewed efforts to reduce illegal entries." To this end, the commission made extensive, detailed recommendations.

The commision's key recommendation is for a computerized verification system that would enable employers to quickly and accurately check that a social security number is valid and has been issued to someone authorized to work in the United States. The commission reported that "reducing the employment magnet is the linchpin of a comprehensive strategy to reduce illegal immigration." A computer registry of eligible workers would make the IRCA more effective. The commission proposes a test of such a system in five states with large illegal immigrant populations.

The commission recommended that public agencies use the same computerized verification system to check an individual's eligibility for social service benefits. This would enable the government to consistently enforce eligibility requirements and eliminate misuse of public services by illegal immigrants.

President Clinton has taken the commission's recommendations into consideration in issuing a 1995 budget proposal that increases funding to the INS and adds seven hundred border patrol agents. These funds are part of a strategy to "control the border and bring the INS into the 21st century before the 21st century," said U.S. attorney general Janet Reno. The proposal includes funds to reimburse some state governments for health, education, and incarceration expenses for illegal immigrants. Also, money has been set aside for trial computerized verification programs similar to the one recommended by the commission. The president further pledged to punish employers who hire illegal immigrants by seeking federal authority "to confiscate assets that are the fruits of that unfair competition." The commission's report and the Clinton administration's budget proposal seek to solve the problem of illegal immigration with more technology, more manpower, and more effective enforcement.

Enhancing enforcement

Some experts continue to support enforcement as the key to halting illegal immigration. David Simcox, executive director of the Center for Immigration Studies in Washington, says:

> With each cost and risk factor—more border patrol agents, tighter enforcement of employer sanctions, greater use of sensors, additional fences—there is a fraction that won't take the risk. If we decrease the number by half, the impact over a decade would be tremendous.

Perhaps this is true. California senator Dianne Feinstein introduced a bill in 1994 to add twenty-one hundred more border patrol agents, create a fraud-proof ID card, and double the penalty for smuggling immigrants. Feinstein proposes to finance these expansions with a $1 toll on all border crossings.

Another proposal would assign ten thousand military personnel to back up the border patrol. Opponents argue that sending the military to the border looks like war and that the United States is not at war with Mexico. But proponents of stronger deterrents agree with California governor Pete Wilson who has said, "We can no longer allow compassion to overrule reason."

Increased enforcement efforts may temporarily stabilize the flow of people across the border, but the real solution to illegal immigration may lie in political and economic changes in other countries.

Higher walls and better tracking of illegal immigrants may actually have little effect. That approach attacks the plant without touching the roots. Experts point out that enforcement will never reduce the flow of people. It will only, at best, stabilize it. "If the US really wants to keep

people out, they need to do it like East Germany did and put soldiers every 10 feet and shoot people—but even then, we'll go," says Carlos Rivera, about to set out for the United States. Enforcement can become more forceful and encompass a greater area, but people will find a way to come over the border illegally.

Political and economic solutions

Those who urge political and economic solutions point to the overall failure of enforcement programs. As things are progressing now, the number of illegal immigrants continues to increase. "Washington and Mexico City cannot continue to look at immigration as a law enforcement problem, but must work to seek political solutions. If they don't, Mexico's chief export will continue to be capital, people, and drugs," says Primitivo Rodriguez, spokesman for the United States–Mexico Border Program.

Many immigration experts look to NAFTA, the North American Free Trade Agreement, as an important, long-term solution. NAFTA is an international trade agreement between the United States, Canada, and Mexico. The object of this agreement is to eliminate trade barriers between the three nations and reduce the cost of doing business. The expected result is economic growth in each country, new export markets, increased investment, and higher wages. "The current levels of illegal migration are not inevitable. What happens on the Mexican side is what will determine the flow," says Wayne Cornelius of UCSD. As Mexican wages rise, experts predict that illegal immigration will fall. "Free trade is not a quick fix, but it is not going to take decades. I think you could see some significant improvement in 5 to 10 years," says Cornelius. Some experts stretch the timetable to two generations.

Another solution is to change present immigration law from the focus on family preference and job skills to a first-come first-served lottery. This would give everyone an equal chance at legal immigration. Applicants would be reviewed by filing order in each country. To avoid domination by countries with large populations, no country's annual quota could exceed a certain percentage of the total. This system would be completely objective and fair and give everyone the same opportunity at legal immigration. As the laws stand now, many people around the world know they do not have a chance to migrate legally; so they abandon the effort and come illegally.

Should America invite foreign workers?

If America acted on its needs for cheap migrant labor another solution is at hand. The government could establish a guest-worker program similar to the *Bracero* program of the 1940s and invite people to come here to work. Employers who seek to hire migrant workers would be able to fill their jobs. Many politicians and experts support this idea, including California attorney general Dan Lungren, who pointed out:

> The reality is in this century we've had a flow of labor from Mexico, legal or illegal, depending on what laws we have at the time. If people try to say there aren't illegal workers out there in agriculture and in other industries, they are deceiving themselves. What I'm saying is that instead of trying to pretend it doesn't exist, why not regularize it?

Migration experts express concern that such a program might result in exploitation of workers through substandard housing, low wages, and no benefits. Although these conditions are already common for migrant workers, the workers are not part of a government-sponsored program. "The fundamental problem I have is we invite people

into this country to take advantage of their labor, but we don't allow them to enjoy this society," said Mike Hancock, director of the Farmworker Justice Fund in Washington, D.C.

Consideration, discussion, and support of a guest-worker program has been growing, yet no formal proposals have been made. "I guess a guest worker program might be part of the solution (to illegal immigration). But we have to stress that we haven't seen a clear proposal yet," said Miguel Ruiz-Cabanas, minister of social and border affairs of the Mexican embassy in Washington, D.C.

One suggestion for halting illegal immigration is to reestablish a Bracero-type program. Some experts worry that such a program would lead to an increase in substandard housing similar to the crowded quarters in which these Haitians live in North Carolina.

Open Borders

A few experts address the possibility of completely open borders. In the 1980s the *Wall Street Journal* ran editorials urging an end to limits on immigration.

WOULD YOU WANT TO LIVE IN A HOUSE WITHOUT DOORS?

If Washington still wants to "do something" about immigration, we propose a five-word consitutional amendment: There shall be open borders....This nation needs the rejuvenation that recurrent waves of new Americans bring. Latins, Vietnamese and West Indians are the new Irish, Italians and Poles.

America could be a country without boundaries or immigration limits. Anyone who wanted to come, could come. The only requirements would be that, once here, they must obey American laws. There would be no INS and no border patrol. The money could be put toward other uses.

Although most Americans are uncomfortable with the idea of uncontrolled borders, America's history shows that prosperity follows immigration. Economists point out that the economic boom of the 1950s and 1960s was driven by immigration and that the Depression of the 1930s began after the restrictive Immigration Act of 1924 was implemented. "One of the causes of the depression was a sharp reduction in demand for housing and consumer goods beginning in about 1926–27. . . . Had we maintained immigration at the levels of the early 1920s . . . consumption would have been substantially higher," explains economist Dr. Thomas Muller.

Proponents of open borders point to Europe as an example of how the program can work well. In 1957 free movement of labor was authorized everywhere within the boundaries of the European Economic Community. Many citizens and officials of northern European countries were opposed to the policy because they feared large numbers of poor immigrants from southern countries would overcrowd their cities and take jobs away from locals. This never happened. "Legalizing immigration for EEC citizens had remarkably little effect on the total number of people moving across the border," said Barbara Nolan, an Irish official. Only a small percentage of people are willing to give up their familiar life for an unknown life in a strange country.

> The real controls are complicated things like cultural traditions and language, not the physical barriers between countries. This is why our free-circulation policy has not resulted in large movements of people, despite very large differentials within the EU in living standards and wages.

In fact, European Union (as the EEC is now called) officials say that unhindered movement of goods, services, and people across borders is essential to the economic success of all the member countries. American proponents of this idea point out that open borders would enhance the beneficial effects of NAFTA as well as help solve the problem of illegal immigration.

What kind of society do Americans want?

Americans who accept illegal immigration as a fact of life in the United States argue that the important issue is not how many undocumented workers there are or whether they help or hurt the

American economy, but how Americans treat illegal immigrants. What effect does an exploited underclass have on America? Paying illegal immigrants low wages and working them long hours goes against everything that American labor unions have sought to achieve over the years. "The problem is not that illegals are taking jobs. The problem is what they are getting paid and (their) working conditions," says Muzaffar Chishti of the Ladies' Garment Workers' Union.

Many communities have begun to accept the presence of illegal immigrants and to establish programs to assist them. Officials in the Orange County, California, communities of Brea and Laguna Beach designated specific sites for day laborers and potential employers to congregate. These sites serve all job seekers, regardless of im-

Like this Guatemalan family, many immigrants have sought a new life in the United States. The attraction of political freedom and economic opportunity is strong enough to keep legal and illegal immigrants coming to America.

migration status. A telephone job-referral service was set up in Dana Point to assist day laborers, regardless of immigration status. Volunteers answer telephones and try to match laborers with employers looking for workers. "Each city has to take care of the problem in its own backyard. The federal government can't possibly handle it all," said Hector Valles, a retired furniture manufacturer who coordinates the Dana Point program.

Immigrants, both legal and illegal, have always been a part of this country. How Americans choose to cope with the illegal immigrants in their midst reflects the kind of society Americans intend to create for themselves. America can turn its back to the world and ignore those illegal immigrants who are already in the country. Or America can accept its place as a country that offers freedom and opportunity and learn to accommodate everyone who desires to be here.

Organizations
to Contact

The following list of organizations represents a mixture of immigrant advocates and opponents. Each one generates facts and statistics to support its particular viewpoint. It is useful to be aware of an organization's bias when reading its publications.

American Civil Liberties Union (ACLU)
132 W. 43rd St.
New York, NY 10036
(212) 944-9800
fax: (212) 921-7916

The ACLU protects the individual rights granted by the Declaration of Independence and the U.S. Constitution. Its Immigrant's Rights Project supports refugees and immigrants with deportation or workplace problems. Along with studies and reports, the ACLU has published a book, *The Rights of Aliens and Refugees*, which details the constitutionally granted rights available to refugees and aliens.

American Friends Service Committee (AFSC)
1501 Cherry St.
Philadelphia, PA 19102
(215) 241-7000

The Quaker-run AFSC lobbies against unfair or discriminatory immigration laws and promotes the Quaker values of peace, nonviolence, and justice. The AFSC has published a book, *Sealing Our Borders: The Human Toll*, which documents violations of human rights by law enforcement agents against immigrants.

American Immigration Control Foundation (AICF)
Box 525
Main St.
Monterey, VA 24465
(703) 468-2022
fax: (703) 468-2024

The AICF is a private organization of American citizens concerned about the effects of immigration, especially illegal immigration, on America. The organization seeks to educate Americans about the need for immigration control. It also conducts research to find resolutions to what it perceives as the current illegal immigration crisis. Publications include a newsletter titled *Border Watch*, as well as pamphlets.

Americans for Immigration Control (AIC)
717 Second St. NE, Suite 307
Washington, DC 20002
(202) 543-3719

The AIC lobbies for increases in the budget for the INS and border patrol, use of military forces to assist the border patrol, and stiff sanctions against employers who knowingly hire illegal immigrants.

Americas Watch (AW)
485 Fifth Ave.
New York, NY 10017
(212) 972-8400
fax: (212) 972-0905

AW, a human rights organization, protects human rights, especially for Latin Americans. It seeks to reduce human rights violations by publicizing abuses and organizing international protests against the government responsible. Among their publications is *Brutality Unchecked: Human Rights Abuses Along the US Border with Mexico*.

Center for Immigrants Rights (CIR)
48 St. Marks Place, 4th Floor
New York, NY 10003
(212) 505-6890
fax: (212) 995-5876

The CIR offers technical assistance, training, and education in immigration law for church, community, and labor organizations. It provides immigrants with information regarding their rights, legal support, and advocacy and seeks to influence immigration law. Its publications include the *CIR Report*, which is issued quarterly, and the *Advocates Manual for Immigrant Health Access*.

Center for Immigration Studies
1815 H St. NW, Suite 101
Washington, DC 20006
(202) 466-8185

The center studies the effects of immigration on all aspects of life in the United States. It advocates reforming immigration laws to decrease the perceived burden of immigration. Its publications include *Scope*, a quarterly journal.

Emergency Committee to Suspend Immigration
P.O. Box 1211
Marietta, GA 30061
(404) 422-1180

A private organization that seeks to suspend all non-European immigration. It supports the view that non-European immigrants, both legal and illegal, cause many problems, including those created by drugs, in the United States.

Federation for American Immigration Reform (FAIR)
1666 Connecticut Ave. NW, Suite 400
Washington, DC 20009
(202) 328-7004
fax: (202) 387-3447

FAIR supports strict limits on legal immigration and efforts to stop illegal immigration. It advocates better enforcement along U.S. borders and careful visa monitoring. It encourages leaders of countries with overpopulation and weak economies to stop emigration. Publications include a newsletter *FAIR Immigration Report* and the bimonthly *FAIR Information Exchange*.

Immigration and Naturalization Service (INS)
425 I St. NW
Washington, DC 20536
(202) 514-2547 information resources
(202) 514-1900 commissioner's office
fax: (202) 514-3296

The INS, in the Department of Justice, enforces and regulates immigration law. Publications include *Statistical Yearbook of the INS, INS Fact Book,* and *An Immigrant Nation: US Regulation of Immigration, 1798–1991.*

Immigration and Refugee Services of America (IRSA)
1717 Massachusetts Ave. NW, Suite 701
Washington, DC 20036
(202) 797-2105

The IRSA assists refugees and immigrants in adjusting to life in America and promotes multiculturalism.

The Mexico–United States Institute (MUSI)
1910 K St. NW, Suite 402
Washington, DC 20006
(202) 775-8560

MUSI studies, researches, and analyzes U.S.–Mexican relations. It has published *Illegal Immigration: An Unfolding Crisis.*

National Immigration Forum
220 I St. NE, Suite 220
Washington, DC 20002
(202) 544-0004
fax: (202) 544-1905

This coalition defends the rights of immigrants and helps the communities in which they settle. It provides communication between local and national organizations, discussion on immigrant issues and strategies, research, and policy analysis. Its publications include several newsletters: *Action Alert, Advocacy Matters,* and *EPIC Events.*

National Immigration Law Center (NILC)
1636 W. 8th St., Suite 215
Los Angeles, CA 90017
(213) 487-2531
fax: (213) 384-4899

The NILC serves as a national center for immigrant and refugee issues. It conducts training and research and operates as an advocate for immigrants and refugees.

National Network for Immigrant and Refugee Rights (NNIRR)
310 8th St., No. 307
Oakland, CA 94607
(510) 465-1984
fax: (510) 465-7548

The NNIRR defends, advocates, and organizes for immigrant and refugee rights. It supports fair immigration policy and compiles statistics. Its newsletter, *Network News*, is published monthly.

Suggestions for Further Reading

Ted Conover, *Coyotes: A Journey Through the Secret World of America's Illegal Aliens.* New York: Vintage, 1987.

————, "Chasing the Dream," *Scholastic Update*, November 19, 1993.

Myles Gordon, "Golden Door," *Scholastic Update*, November 19, 1993.

Pierre N. Hauser, *Illegal Aliens.* New York: Chelsea House Publishers, 1990.

Donna R. Plesser, Mark A. Siegel, and Carol D. Foster, eds. *Immigration and Illegal Aliens: Burden or Blessing?* Plano, TX: Information Aids, Inc., 1989.

Ken Silverstein, "The Labor Debate," *Scholastic Update*, November 19, 1993.

Works Consulted

Jennifer Allen, "Fly North," *The New Republic*, December 27, 1993.

William Barbour, ed., *Illegal Immigration*. San Diego: Greenhaven Press, 1994.

James Bornemeier, "Clinton Moves to Curb Illegal Immigration," *Los Angeles Times*, February 8, 1995.

Raoul Lowery Contreras, "Slaughter Alley," *Reason*, June 1991.

Mary H. Cooper, "Immigration Reform," *The CQ Researcher*, September 24, 1993.

Juanita Darling, "Migrants' Social, Economic Ties to Mexico Stay Strong," *Los Angeles Times*, November 29, 1993.

Brian Duffy, "Coming to America," *U.S. News & World Report*, June 21, 1993.

The Economist, "American Survey: At America's Door," July 24, 1993.

Susan Ferriss, "Should U.S. Invite Mexican Workers?" *San Francisco Examiner*, February 12, 1995.

Glenn Garvin, "America's Economic Refugees," *Reason*, November 1993.

Paul Glastis, "Immigration Crackdown," *U.S. News & World Report*, June 21, 1993.

Nathan Glazer, "The Closing Door," *The New Republic*, March 22, 1993.

Rodman D. Griffin, "Illegal Immigration," *The CQ Researcher*, April 24, 1992.

Donald Huddle, "The Net National Costs of Immigration," July 20, 1993; a report by the Carrying Capacity Network.

Daniel James, *Illegal Immigration: An Unfolding Crisis*. Lanham, MD: University Press of America, 1991.

Jesse Katz, "The Hopes, Fears and Struggles," *Los Angeles Times*, November 28, 1993.

Dianne Klein, "A Hit or Miss Approach to Curbing Deportable Felons," *Los Angeles Times*, November 27, 1993.

Robert Kuttner, "Illegal Immigration: Would a National ID Card Help?" *Business Week*, August 26, 1991.

Melinda Liu, "How to Play the Asylum Game," *Newsweek*, August 2, 1993.

———, "The New Slave Trade," *Newsweek*, June 21, 1993.

Joe Maxwell, "The Alien in Our Midst," *Christianity Today*, December 13, 1993.

Alan C. Miller, "Data Sheds Heat, Little Light on Immigration Debate," *Los Angeles Times*, November 21, 1993.

Debbie Nathan, "A Death on the Border," *The Progressive*, March 1993.

National Catholic Reporter, "Military Erects 'Berlin Wall' on Mexican Border," September 6, 1991.

Bruce W. Nelan, "Not Quite So Welcome Anymore," *Time*, Fall 1993.

The New Yorker, Talk of the Town: "La Pupusa Loca," March 1, 1993.

Richard A. Parker and Louis M. Rea, *Illegal Immigration in San Diego County: An Analysis of Costs and Revenues, Report to the California State Senate Committee on Border Issues*. Sacramento, CA: Senate Publications, 1993.

James Popkin and Dorian Friedman, "Return to Sender, Please," *U.S. News & World Report*, June 21, 1992.

Larry Rohter, "Florida Wants Aid for Illegal Immigrants," *The New York Times*, December 31, 1993.

Richard Simon, "Illegal Residents Not Just from Nearby Nations," *Los Angeles Times*, November 26, 1993.

Jill Smolowe, "Where's the Promised Land?" *Time*, June 21, 1993.

Bill Turque et al., "Why Our Borders Are Out of Control," *Newsweek*, August 9, 1993.

U.S. Commission on Immigration Reform, *US Immigration Policy: Restoring Credibility, a Report to Congress*, September 1994.

U.S. Department of Justice, Immigration and Naturalization Service, *An Immigrant Nation: United States Regulation of Immigration, 1798–1991*, June 18, 1991.

U.S. Department of Justice, Immigration and Naturalization Service, *1992 Statistical Yearbook of the Immigration and Naturalization Service*, October 1993.

Frank Viviano, "Borders Without Patrols," *San Francisco Chronicle*, February 19, 1995.

Index

About the Author

Kathleen Lee is the author of *Tracing Our Italian Roots*, a children's book about Italian immigration to America. She is a freelance writer living in Santa Fe, New Mexico. She holds a degree in British and American literature from Scripps College in Claremont, California.

Picture Credits

Cover photo: David Maung/Impact Visuals
AP/Wide World Photos, 15, 23, 26, 83, 84, 98
David Bacon/Impact Visuals, 58
The Bettmann Archive, 20, 52, 95
Chris Cavanaugh/*The San Diego Union*, 62, 63
Nelvin Cepeda/*The San Diego Union-Tribune*, 60
Philip Decker/Impact Visuals, 43
Dana Fisher/*The San Diego Union-Tribune*, 74
Michelle Gienow/Impact Visuals, 92, 96
Imagen Latina/Impact Visuals, 79
Sue M. Johnson/Impact Visuals, 48
Mike Kamber/Impact Visuals, 36
Library of Congress, 12
Ken Martin/Impact Visuals, 110
Tom McKitterick/Impact Visuals, 28
Reuters/Bettmann, 22, 56, 88, 91
Jeffry D. Scott/Impact Visuals, 6, 30, 66, 69, 80, 104
Christopher Takagi/Impact Visuals, 72
Adam Taylor/Impact Visuals, 99
Philip True/Impact Visuals, 38
Jim West/Impact Visuals, 9, 35
UPI/Bettmann, 10, 16, 18, 25, 33, 46, 76, 107